The Gender Issue

ISSUES

Volume 64

Editor

Craig Donnellan

Independence

Educational Publishers
Cambridge

First published by Independence
PO Box 295
Cambridge CB1 3XP
England

British Library Cataloguing in Publication Data
The Gender Issue – (Issues Series)
I. Donnellan, Craig II. Series
331.1'33

ISBN 1 86168 240 9

Printed in Great Britain
MWL Print Group Ltd

Typeset by
Claire Boyd

Cover
The illustration on the front cover is by
Pumpkin House.

CONTENTS

Introduction

The Gender Issue is the sixty-fourth volume in the **Issues** series. The aim of this series is to offer up-to-date information about important issues in our world.

The Gender Issue examines the gender debate in education, the workplace and the home.

The information comes from a wide variety of sources and includes:
Government reports and statistics
Newspaper reports and features
Magazine articles and surveys
Web site material
Literature from lobby groups
and charitable organisations.

It is hoped that, as you read about the many aspects of the issues explored in this book, you will critically evaluate the information presented. It is important that you decide whether you are being presented with facts or opinions. Does the writer give a biased or an unbiased report? If an opinion is being expressed, do you agree with the writer?

The Gender Issue offers a useful starting-point for those who need convenient access to information about the many issues involved. However, it is only a starting-point. At the back of the book is a list of organisations which you may want to contact for further information.

*****

Gender

Information from Save the Children

Boys and girls are born biologically different. But after birth, other differences between the two sexes are created by society. These are called gender differences, and they often lead to unequal opportunities – particularly for girls and women.

What's the problem?

Girls and women, boys and men, are expected to behave in different ways. They are also expected to look, dress, and relate to each other differently, and only do certain types of work. We learn these so-called gender roles as we grow up.

They vary from one culture to another in different parts of the world. But little girls are usually expected to be passive and obedient, play with their dolls, and help their mothers around the house, while boys are supposed to be tough and brave, take risks, get into fights, and not help out at home. This could sound harmless, but it leads to problems later.

In many cultures men and boys are considered to be superior to women and girls. This is called

gender discrimination or gender inequality. Girls typically get less to eat, have to leave school earlier, and are more vulnerable to sexual abuse and exploitation. In later life, the differences become even more obvious. Women usually work longer hours for less pay than men get, have fewer rights, less power, less say, and less access to resources like money, credit, land, jobs, housing and education.

Girls and women, boys and men, are expected to behave in different ways. They are also expected to look, dress, and relate to each other differently

---

- Women do two-thirds of the world's work, but only earn one-tenth of its total income.
- Women own less than one per cent of the world's property.
- Two-thirds of all illiterate people on earth are women.

These United Nations figures add up to wasted potential, shattered hopes and injustice for more than half of the world's population.

So is it just a girls' problem?

No. Gender inequality hurts boys and men too. Boys can be damaged by other people's beliefs about how men should behave. They often learn to solve problems or express anger through violence, which puts them at risk of attack and of hurting people close to them. Many are brought up to think they are naturally superior to girls and therefore don't need to put much effort into achieving success. One result is that more boys under-achieve at school than girls.

So what's the solution?

Empowerment is a crucial way to tackle inequality. This is about boys and girls, men and women taking

control of their own lives, making their own decisions, gaining new skills and self-confidence, solving problems and relying on themselves. For example, there is no point in just giving poor women an extra job. They could just end up working even harder than before, with someone else controlling the extra money they earn.

But if they've been able to develop their self-confidence and skills they can start to challenge unequal power relations in their community.

Where Save the Children stands

We fight all forms of discrimination and believe that all children have the right to achieve their potential regardless of their circumstances. We want both girls and boys to fulfil their potential and become active citizens, and this involves challenging gender inequality.

Our work is underpinned by an international law called the United Nations Convention on the Rights of the Child (UNCRC), which says governments must grant a list of 54 rights to all children, regardless of sex. Save the Children also uses another convention that outlaws discrimination against women to promote children's rights.

Women are the main child carers in most societies. If your mother is poor, sick, has little confidence, no say, and maybe has a husband who beats her, then your chances of becoming a healthy, fulfilled adult are much lower. Supporting and empowering mothers is therefore an important way of helping children.

Save the Children fights all forms of discrimination and believes that all children have the right to achieve their potential regardless of their circumstances

---

Gender work is not a separate area of Save the Children's work – it cuts across all the different issues and projects we work on. In particular, we focus on violence, girls' rights, and boys' gender identity.

Here are some examples of Save the Children projects that tackle gender inequality.

- In the UK, we have supported several projects to combat domestic violence. Training manuals and a video for those working with young people challenge gender stereotypes, aim to raise awareness of the effects of violence on under-18s, and improve how the sexes relate to each other.
- Nepalese girls can't move about freely, because many public areas are considered unsafe and going out is not seen to be respectable. We work with girls to identify and reclaim 'safe spaces'.
- We also support a local organisation which has rescued many girls

from sex traffickers, and trained them to become activists and awareness raisers.
- In Uzbekistan, we support a Mothers' and Daughters' School which teaches women new professional skills and to speak out on issues that concern them, and educates girls who have suffered abuse or been in trouble with the law.
- We recently took part in a UK education campaign to encourage fathers to read to their sons. The aim was to improve boys' reading and writing, strengthen fathers' roles, and spread the idea that reading books isn't just for girls.
- In Uganda, an HIV/Aids project enables girls to promote positive sexual behaviour, increase knowledge and understanding of how HIV/Aids affects children, and encourage communities to get more involved in caring for children affected by Aids. Our support groups for girls are educational, and lead to boosting their self-esteem and confidence.
- Want to find out more about Save the Children and our work? If you have access to the Internet, visit www.savethechildren.org.uk/rightonline or send us your thoughts by e-mailing yep@scfuk.org.uk or by writing to Education Unit, Save the Children, 17 Grove Lane, London, SE5 8RD. Tel: 020 7703 5400.

© Save the Children

Young women and education

Equality is learned

The facts

Education, the driving force behind equality

Education provides an opportunity to 'learn' about equality between women and men. Non-sexist education makes it possible very early on to attack traditional stereotypes concerning the roles of women and men and to fight prejudice and discrimination. The young women in the network all agree that *appropriate education can correct many of the stereotypes that support the inequalities that women face.* Education and training is also the key to women's access to the job market.

European girls and women nonetheless still encounter more obstacles than men do concerning access to education, recognition of their abilities in the education system (by teachers when they are pupils and by their hierarchy when they become teachers) and finding a job. Education, which should be the driving force behind equality of opportunity, often reproduces discrimination between women and men.

The problem is not only one of discrimination, but of a loss to European society as a whole, which is depriving itself of the intellectual potential of half its population especially at a time when Europe must prove its ability to compete on the world market.

A few statistics

- Only 45% of participants in education and vocational training are female.
- Only 4% of university chairs are occupied by women in Austria, compared to 10% in Italy, 12.8% in Finland and 13% in France.[1]
- Women by far out-perform men at school and university, but they still have more difficulty finding a job; in the European Union, 21% of young women are unemployed as opposed to 18.2% of young men.[2]

A right refused to some young women

Traditionally, for minority ethnic groups, education has represented a chance for integration, for choices and for social advancement, a tool for access to success based on merit. But in some communities, access to education for girls and young women is a real problem: education is not considered a high priority for girls, who are neither supported nor encouraged in the pursuit of their studies, if they are not prohibited outright from studying. Migrant or ethnic-minority parents of young girls are sometimes not well informed about the workings of the education systems. For these young girls, education is therefore not always a right.

The law

The European Union has launched major European education programmes, all of which emphasise equality between women and men.

- Youth: the largest youth policy programme, encompassing youth exchanges and European voluntary services.
- Leonardo: this programme, dedicated to vocational training,

---

Only 4% of university chairs are occupied by women in Austria, compared to 10% in Italy, 12.8% in Finland and 13% in France

---

provides opportunities for learning and career development in other countries.

- Socrates supports European cooperation in all areas related to education and has made equality between women and men a criterion for selection.

Young women's ideas

The young women propose specific ideas for making each link in the education chain contribute to equality between women and men:

- Raising the awareness not only of pupils, but also of teachers, school staff members and parents concerning male-female equality.
- Using non-sexist language in all educational materials (for example, 'chair person' instead of 'chairman') to attack the discrimination inherent in everyday language.
- Encouraging lifelong learning and facilitating the resumption of studies, particularly for young women who have had to interrupt them due to pregnancy.
- Training teachers and students in women's history and on the theme of equality between women and men.

References

1 Notes from the 'Women and Science' Conference of 28-29 April 1998, European Commission
2 *The social situation in the EU 2000*, Eurostat – European Commission

- The above information is an extract from *Young Women's Guide to Equality between Women and Men in Europe*, a publication by the European Women's Lobby. See page 41 for their address details or visit their web site: www.womenlobby.org

The lads in a league of their own

Macho culture may be the norm – but boys can still score academically. Fred Redwood reports on a comprehensive success story

You can tell the naughty boys by their eyes. Furtive and in search of mischief, the boys come into their French lesson with a nudge here, a trip there, a whisper from the corner of the mouth. But Peta Parsons, their teacher, has their measure.

Speaking only in French, she commands the boys to stand at their desks. 'Asseyez-vous' – they sit. 'Levez-vous' – they stand. The orders are given and followed five times. Then, while standing, each boy has to deliver a clear, grammatically correct sentence about his plans for the weekend before receiving permission to sit down and wait in silence for the lesson to begin.

Far from being a description of a strict, old-fashioned teacher, this is an example of the carefully planned strategies that have dramatically improved the performance of boys at King's School, a coeducational comprehensive in Winchester, Hampshire, for 11- to 16-year-olds.

Its first attempts at redressing boys' under-achievement were reported four years ago. In 1998, 69 per cent of boys gained at least five GCSEs at grades A to C compared with 73 per cent of girls. That was a vast improvement on two years earlier, when only 55 per cent of boys achieved the benchmark, compared with 77 per cent of girls.

'Give most girls a map to copy and they'll do it, Boys will question the point of the exercise and volunteer to go to the photocopier'

This year, the boys at King's have actually overtaken the girls: 82 per cent gained five top grades, compared with 79 per cent of girls. How has such a transformation come about?

'We have taken the "laddish" culture of our boys and, instead of quashing it, we have harnessed it to good effect,' says Ray Bradbury, the head.

'Boys get as much praise in assembly for their sporting achievements, for example, as do the girls for their gentler pursuits. Successful old boys are invited in to talk about the importance of doing well, and we create an atmosphere of encouragement for boys as well as girls.

'Writing snide, negative comments on boys' reports, which used to be a staff-room sport in some schools, is unacceptable here, because boys have feelings, too.

'Most importantly, we have identified the boys who are in danger of under-achieving and we teach them in single-sex groups in English, maths and French, using methods specially adapted for those who can be "a bit of a handful".'

Ms Parsons, the head of French, is an expert practitioner of these methods. Once her boys are settled, they work on tasks in short bursts. In the lesson I watched, they were given French phrases and had to write and rehearse sketches, and then perform them to the class. All were involved, either acting or correcting each other's pronunciation, and there was no sign of self-consciousness.

An atmosphere of good-natured 'joshing' and mickey-taking is allowed, within clearly defined boundaries. One boy who deliberately hammed up his sketch, probably for my benefit, was immediately moved to work alone – there are no second chances.

Finally, after warm praise – 'You are all absolutely brilliant at speaking French' – the boys were allowed to leave, but only after they had each announced, 'J'aime le français' as they went out of the door.

'These boys are bright, lively and funny and I love teaching them,' says Ms Parsons. 'But they won't plan long term like the more mature girls and, consequently, if they are given, say, a 250-word assignment, they won't get round to it. However, if I divide it into 50-word segments, they will work quite happily.

'Boys have a fiercely competitive streak, which I draw upon. On the wall are football-style league tables representing marks in vocabulary tests. Competing to be top of the league spurs them on tremendously.'

'Another laddish trait is the need for constant encouragement, so I try to make them feel valued and liked. They are also more questioning of the tasks they receive. Give most girls a map to copy and they'll do it. Boys will question the point of the exercise and volunteer to go to the photocopier. That's why I always recap at the end of the lesson, summarising the ground we have covered.'

The boys appear to enjoy the lesson. With disarming honesty, one says: 'I have more fun in my mixed lessons, but I learn more when I'm with the lads. In mixed classes, girls get all the attention by being brainy, so I get it back by being bad.'

Is segregation within the mainstream desirable, or does it merely pander to macho yobbishness?

Rob Jekyll, the English teacher at Kings', who is responsible for the co-ordination of boys' achievement, says: 'We adapt the system for the needs of boys in the same way as we would adapt it for pupils with a specific learning difficulty. The girls also benefit because potentially troublesome boys are removed from their classes.

'The boys' class is not dependent on having a male teacher – women teachers are often better with them. But you do need someone in charge who is firm, methodical and quick-witted.'

Even allowing for grade inflation, the improvement in Kings' GCSE results over the past seven years has been remarkable. In 1995, 50 per cent of all pupils gained at least five grades A to C; this year, 81 per cent did so.

The proportion of boys achieving at least a grade C in French rose from 59 per cent last year to 77 per cent this year, when the first boys-only class was introduced.

It will be interesting to see if other schools learn from these lessons.

© Telegraph Group Limited, London 2003

Understanding G & A

The 'rough guide' to gender and achievement

Boys' underachievement is a major concern. Nationally, boys fall behind girls in early literacy skills and this gap in attainment is sustained over time. Of course that's not the whole story, many boys are doing well at school, whilst some girls are failing to reach their full potential too.

Because tackling underachievement is such a complex issue and no two schools are the same, each school needs to develop its own individual strategies, taking into account the character of the local community and the unique blend of its students.

Key points

The standards of achievement for all pupils has been rising since the 1980s but because of the differential rates of improvements, girls are still performing better than boys

Boys are interpreted as underachieving because overall their crude results (for example A*-Cs) are below that of girls. This pattern is not true for all boys, or for all subjects and differs if we look at progress rather than outcomes (through value added data). The crucial point is in ensuring that policies designed to improve boys' results do not do so at the expense of girls

Boys' underachievement is an international problem. We know for example that in the USA, Australia, Scotland and Holland girls appear to get off to a better start in reading and writing and sustain the advantage in later schooling.

Many boys perform as well as girls. Some girls also underachieve at school. But overall, more boys are low performers. While gender is one of the key factors affecting educational performance, it affects different sub-groups of boys and girls in different ways. Social class, ethnic origin and local context are all factors that may be linked to performance.

Research suggests that the most popular strategies to tackle underachievement include: creating a positive ethos that counters macho anti-school attitudes among boys; literacy strategies targeted at boys' preferred learning styles; performance data analysis and pupil monitoring; the use of mentors and role models and pupil grouping including single-sex teaching for short periods in some subjects. However, most schools use more than one strategy and there is little evidence to suggest that a one-size-fits-all strategy would be effective in all schools.

■ The above information is from the Department for Education and Skills' Standards web site: www.standards.dfes.gov.uk

© 2003 Crown Copyright

The boys are left standing as GCSE gender gap grows

Girls have forged even further ahead in the GCSE battle of the sexes, dashing hopes that boys were at last beginning to catch up.

Results posted in schools in August 2002 showed girls outperformed their male classmates in almost every subject.

They even triumphed in the traditionally male subject of Information Technology, with 64.4 per cent achieving grades A* to C against 55.7 per cent of boys.

Girls now gain more A* grades in every subject, apart from maths and physics

Girls now gain more A* grades in every subject, apart from maths and physics, while opening up huge leads of 14 points or more in art, English literature and languages.

Across all subjects girls stretched to a nine-percentage-point lead, prompting exam chiefs to call for a detailed inquiry into boys' underachievement.

By Laura Clark and Sarah Harris

Overall GCSE pass rates continued their relentless rise, with 57.9 per cent passed at grades A* to C compared to 57.1 per cent in 2001. It was the biggest yearly rise since 1995.

The figures mean the proportion of exams passed at grade C or above has risen since GCSEs were introduced in 1988. The percentage passed at A* has more than doubled since the grade started in 1994.

It had been hoped that boys would narrow the gender gap further this year after taking a bite out of the girls' lead for the first time in 2001. Teachers have been trying to tackle an anti-school 'lad culture'.

But there were mounting calls last night for an investigation into the deeper causes of the problem.

Heads warned that the Government did not have a 'cat in hell's chance' of hitting GCSE performance targets if boys continued to 'drag down' results.

The largest classroom union, the National Union of Teachers, called for a 'thorough review'.

Higher Education Minister Margaret Hodge admitted the attainment divide was 'worryingly high', while Tory spokesman Damian Green said: 'Too many boys are turned off learning in schools. We need urgently to improve the courses we offer, particularly to those who have practical skills.'

The figures showed no downturn in the number of exams taken, despite Government moves to encourage brighter pupils to skip GCSEs and move straight on to sixth-form courses.

Schools also appear to be ignoring Ministers' calls for bright youngsters to be fast-tracked to GCSE. Just 2.2 per cent of exams were taken by children of 15 or below rather than the usual 16. The percentage of youngsters gaining at least grade C rose by 1 per cent in English, and by 1.2 per cent in maths, faster than for most subjects.

But the CBI warned that nearly half still fail to achieve C grades in maths, as demanded by employers, and four in ten fail English.

There was no change in the 2.1 per cent of exams rated 'unclassified grades'. As there were even more 16-year-olds this year, even more youngsters than last year will leave school with nothing to show for 11 years of education.

© *The Daily Mail* *August 2002*

Gender and education

Gender and differential achievement in education and training. A research review

Introduction

The Equal Opportunities Commission (EOC) views education as pivotal in the process of achieving equality of opportunity between men and women. The choices made and standards achieved in education and training remain influential for the whole of people's working and social lives.

The Commission conducted an in-house research review in 1998 to look at the available literature on achievement in education and training. Data are rarely available for Great Britain overall as the Scottish secondary system differs from that in England and Wales. Not only is the curriculum different, but a separate system of examinations and qualifications is followed. Thus,

The majority of Science subjects are dominated by boys, the majority of Arts subjects by girls, whereas the Social Sciences are more mixed

Women. Men. Different. Equal.
Equal Opportunities Commission

research relevant to this review generally focuses on the education and qualification system in England and Wales or that in Scotland, as identified in the text. The box on page 9 is devoted to the situation in Scotland.

It is hoped that the Findings from the review will broaden the current debate surrounding achievement to consider not only that, but also the different access, choices, and destinations of young women and men.

Key findings of the review

Compulsory schooling

Girls are noticeably outperforming boys across all areas at the age of seven, and in English at the ages of eleven and fourteen. More boys than girls tend to score at the extremes, either very high or very low.

Despite the National Curriculum, where choice is allowed at GCSE certain subjects continue to show a distinct gender bias. The majority of Science subjects are dominated by boys, the majority of Arts subjects by girls, whereas the Social Sciences are more mixed.

Girls are clearly outperforming boys in most subjects at GCSE and Standard Grade. Both boys and girls have benefited from more varied styles of teaching and assessment, and have improved their performance at GCSE level and equivalent, but girls' performance has increased more rapidly than that of boys.

Choice has been reintroduced to compulsory schooling through the Part One GNVQs in England and Wales. With clearly gender-stereotyped subject areas like health and social care, manufacturing and engineering, there are concerns that young people may be encouraged to make occupational choices far too early, thereby reducing their future employment possibilities.

Care needs to be taken that any measures which seek to improve the performance of one group of pupils are not at the expense of other pupils. For example, boys are known to benefit from more structured and rule-bound lessons than girls, who prefer more discussion-led and collaborative lessons.

Examination achievements

Examination achievements between girls and boys in 2000/01, United Kingdom, per cent

	Girls				Boys			
	England	Wales	Scotland	UK	England	Wales	Scotland	UK
GCSEs and SCE Standard/NQ*	55.4%	55.0%	64.7%	56.5%	44.8%	44.7%	54.2%	45.7%
5 or more grades A*-C or 1-3	23.8%	23.0%	23.0%	23.6%	24.3%	23.6%	28.6%	24.6%
Grades D-G or 4-7 only	16.4%	15.8%	8.1%	15.5%	24.5%	22.1%	12.2%	23.1%
No graded GCSEs/SCEs	4.4%	6.2%	4.3%	4.4%	6.5%	9.6%	5.0%	6.5%
2 or more GCE A levels or 3 or more SCE/NQ Highers**	40.7%	28.8%	45.2%	40.6%	32.7%	21.5%	32.8%	32.1%

* examination achievements of pupils in their last year of compulsory education, England and Wales figures include GNVQ equivalents.

** examination achievements of pupils in schools and students in FE who at the end of the academic year were aged 18-19 in England, 18 in Wales and 17-19 in Northern Ireland as a percentage of the 18-year-old population; and pupils in Years S5/S6 in Scotland as a percentage of the 17-year-old population.

Source: *Regional Trends 37, 2002 edition, Office for National Statistics*

More than four times as many boys than girls were excluded from schools in England in 1996. Black pupils were far more likely to be excluded than White or Asian pupils, possibly due to the different interpretations placed on their behaviour by teaching staff.

Gender is not the only factor influencing achievement in school. Ethnicity and social class are also significant, but unfortunately, most available data do not take more than one variable into account, often due to small sample sizes. The situation with regard to ethnicity is particularly complex.

The GCSE league table in England is headed primarily by single-sex schools, and those that are independent or public. These schools are highly selective: ability and social class are more important factors than the single-sex nature of the schools.

A-levels, Highers and Higher Education

There are clear gender differences in the proportions of men and women studying particular subjects at A-level and in Highers. All Sciences except for Biological Science are dominated by men, whereas all the Arts are dominated by women. As with GCSE, Social Sciences show a mixed gender distribution.

Men and women now perform as well as each other in most subjects at A-level and Highers. In those subjects where men continue to perform better than women, the gender gap is narrowing.

At A-level, a cross-over in patterns of performance is apparent compared with results at GCSE, whereby more men than women achieve higher level grades in certain subjects.

Social background is significantly related to performance at A-level and Highers, with children from professional, associate professional, managerial and technical occupations gaining a higher average score than children from other backgrounds.

In recent years, higher education has experienced an enormous expansion. There are now very similar numbers of men and women

in higher education, but the numbers of women have grown far more rapidly than those of men. From constituting one-third of undergraduates in 1975, women now make up slightly more than one-half.

Further Education and Vocational Training

Young men are more likely to study mathematical sciences, agriculture or engineering and technology and young women are more likely to study subjects allied to medicine, the social sciences or the creative arts. Hairdressing, secretarial studies and health and social care are known as the three 'women's areas' in further education.

Women are more likely than men to study A-levels and Highers through further education. Similar percentages of young women and men now study for GNVQs, but a greater percentage of men than women study for NVQs and other, traditional vocational qualifications. Similar proportions of men and women now participate in Youth Training, complete their training, gain a qualification and find a job. Young women are more likely than men to be working towards a lower level qualification, to be paid an allowance rather than a wage and to be on YT because they could not find a job or join a college course of their choice.

The costs of training to employers vary depending on the type of industry. Substantially more is spent on trainees in sectors which have a tradition of apprenticeships like construction and engineering where the trainees are mainly young men, than on trainees in the hotel and catering industry or local authorities where there is a more even gender balance.

Apprenticeships have always been gender segregated, and those in the Modern Apprenticeship scheme are no exception. Young people were encouraged into areas which already operated an apprenticeship scheme and as a result, traditional gender stereotyping has persisted. Many sectors are strongly gender biased including the two most popular sectors, engineering manufacturing and business administration.

Any attempt to examine vocational training and qualifications is hampered by the lack of accurate data disaggregated by gender. Many official analyses still do not consider gender as a variable.

Men and women participate in different types of postgraduate study. Men are more likely than women to be studying for a higher degree through research or on a taught course, but are less likely to be taking some 'other' form of taught course. Twice as many women than men study for a postgraduate teaching qualification.

Gender stereotyping is as prevalent at degree level as in other qualification levels. Men are over-represented in Engineering and Technology whereas women are over-represented in Education and the Humanities.

In British universities overall, women achieve proportionately more good degrees than men. Men achieve slightly more first class degrees than women, and substantially more third class and pass degrees. A far greater proportion of women achieve an upper second degree. The situation differs in individual institutions, and on average, men at 'Oxbridge' achieve better degrees than women.

Men and women interviewed during their degree courses have

different expectations after graduation. Women are more cautious and tend to underestimate their skills development. They are more likely to take temporary or part-time work than men, and have less considered career plans.

Men with Science, Engineering and Technology degrees are more likely than women to enter management or a professional occupation allied to their degree. Women are more likely than men to enter teaching.

Conclusions

Some children in the compulsory schooling sector, mainly boys, are alienated from education and facing 'social exclusion'. In addition, the subject choices of both boys and girls impact upon their future employment possibilities.

Boys' subject choice excludes them from clerical and caring occupations where many of the new job opportunities exist. And although girls and young women are performing well in examinations at all levels, their subject choice automatically excludes them from scientific and technological professions which require specialisation at an early age.

Certain measures have been shown to improve boys' concentration and performance in individual schools. A 'good practice guide' for practitioners showing what can work would prove invaluable. It is important that any measures should be monitored and evaluated to ensure that all pupils have the opportunity to benefit from their implementation. In addition, there is a need to place the school experience in a wider societal context to address attitudes towards the role of parents and family, education, employ-

---

Boys' subject choice excludes them from clerical and caring occupations where many of the new job opportunities exist

---

Scotland

At the age of 14, pupils in Scotland choose Standard grade subjects from eight curricular modes. Gender stereotyping of choice remains, and is likely to be greater for working class than for middle-class pupils.

Although the average examination performance of boys and girls has increased at Standard grade, girls have progressed more rapidly than boys. Girls are less likely than boys to leave school with no educational qualification.

Traditionally girls have done well in English and they continue to achieve better results than boys in this subject at Standard grade. Despite a steady increase in the numbers of boys taking French and German, girls' performance improved relative to boys in Modern Foreign Languages during the 1990s. Similar numbers of girls and boys take Mathematics and achieve comparable results.

The Standard grade examination enables performance in different elements of a subject to be analysed. Girls tend to do well on internally assessed elements whereas boys' grades are more variable than girls, for example, in problem solving in Science.

The number of school exclusions appears to be very low in Scotland compared with England and Wales. However, this is partly due to the way in which 'exclusion' is defined and the data are collected in Scotland. Gender disaggregated data on the number of exclusions are not collected.

A greater proportion of young women compared with young men stay on in post-compulsory education. Continuing participation is closely linked with educational attainment, gender and social class.

The high attaining group at Standard grade has the highest participation in S5, S6 and HE; the middle attaining group is the most likely to enter FE; and the low attaining group tend to enter Youth Training. Men are more likely than women to enter some form of training.

Overall, a greater percentage of girls than boys leave school with at least one Higher grade. Until the mid 1980s, similar percentages of girls and boys left school with five or more Highers but by the mid 1990s, a five per cent gap had emerged in favour of girls. This is a considerable improvement in girls' performance relative to that of boys'. Overall, however, there is little difference in the average scores of young women and men who take and achieve examinations at Higher grade, unlike the more apparent differences at Standard grade.

The Scottish School Leavers Survey (SSLS) illustrates interesting differences between young women and men and the type of training scheme or job which they enter. Gender stereotyping is clearly apparent. At the time of the last SSLS for which data are currently available (1995), one in three women were in clerical and secretarial jobs/training schemes whereas more than two out of five men were in craft and related jobs/training schemes.

A greater percentage of men than women develop further qualifications through on and off the job training or through a recognised apprenticeship. The Modern Apprenticeship scheme in Scotland has been less influential due in part to the more established nature of Skillseekers. Even so, training opportunities are found mainly in traditionally male dominated sectors.

---

ment, unemployment and individual expectations.

One of the most important omissions is the lack of good quality, accurate data on the qualifications, performance and employment experience of young people disaggregated, at the very least, by gender and preferably also by ethnicity and social class.

■ The above information is an extract from *Gender and Differential Achievement in Education and Training: A Research Review*, ISBN 1 870358 80 5, produced by the Equal Opportunities Commission (EOC). For more recent information, visit their web site at www.eoc.org.uk or see page 41 for their address details.
© *Equal Opportunities Commission (EOC)*

Young women and work

Women are the first victims of flexibility

The facts

Double discrimination

The gap separating men and women on the job market remains wide in all countries of the European Union: women have a lower employment rate, are unemployed longer, are paid less and have less secure jobs. Young women in particular pay the price of job market flexibility. They suffer double discrimination. First, for being young, in the difficult phase of transition between training and working life, in an age group that has, on average, twice the jobless rate of older workers, and at the mercy of employers who exploit them under the pretext of enabling them to acquire professional experience. Secondly they are discriminated against for being women and are more likely to be offered low-paying or low-status jobs. Some groups of young women such as migrant, disabled or lesbian women face even greater difficulties.

Although young women are increasingly choosing typically 'male' professions, they remain over-represented in traditionally 'female' jobs, as secretaries and nurses

---

Women, by a large majority, continue to assume most family responsibilities and resign themselves to accepting part-time jobs that allow them to combine family and work responsibilities. Part-time work limits their potential for career advancement and above all reduces their rights to social security and pension benefits, further aggravating the vulnerability of their situation.

HERE ARE THE TERMS OF YOUR *EMPLOYMENT*—
1. I SAY 'JUMP'
2. YOU ASK 'HOW HIGH?'

Where are the women?

An examination of the breakdown between men and women in each sector of activity shows that discrimination is still very much in evidence and that education and training policies specifically targeting young women are needed to restore a balance. Although young women are increasingly choosing typically 'male' professions, they remain over-represented in traditionally 'female' jobs, as secretaries and nurses, and under-represented in jobs with responsibility and the professions. Neither are women and men represented proportionally in sectors like the information and communication technologies, despite their rapid growth, where women generally occupy positions towards the bottom of the hierarchy. And even in female-dominated sectors like health, women work as nurses, but a large majority of hospital directors and department heads are men.

A few figures

- In the EU as a whole, women doing the same work as a man are paid only 76% of the gross hourly wage men earn;[1]
- The employment rate for women is 51.2%, compared to 70.8% for men.[2]
- 83% of part-time workers in the EU are women.

The law

European legislation concerning equality between women and men in employment is very comprehensive. It covers areas as varied as equality of treatment within social security systems, equal pay, parental leave, application of equality of treatment in relation to access to employment, vocational training and promotion, as well as working conditions and the approximation of Member State laws on equality in many areas. Moreover, since 1997, a person subjected to sex discrimination in the workplace no longer has to prove in court that he or she was indeed the victim of such discrimination, which was generally difficult; it is rather up to the person accused of discrimination to prove it did not take place.

Young women's ideas

Young women's priorities include convincing the European Union's Member States to:

- Extend maternity leave (with better pay) and parental leave (shared with the father); increase the number of affordable childcare facilities, which will support parent's access to the job market.
- Improve the role of trade unions (which remain very male dominated) in favour of young women, in order to challenge invisible discrimination, that is, discrimination that mainly affects women but without targeting them directly and which is often considered gender neutral (such as discrimination against part-time or 'flexible' workers, for example, keeping in mind that the great majority of them are women).
- Encourage the access and promotion of women to positions of responsibility by introducing temporary quotas for women in such jobs.
- Emphasise aid for the creation of enterprises by women for women, to counteract the lack of confidence assistance services show in women entrepreneurs and their lack of confidence in themselves.

References
1 Eurostat, 1999
2 Eurostat, 1998

■ The above information is an extract from *Young Women's Guide to Equality between Women and Men in Europe*, a publication by the European Women's Lobby. See page 41 for their address details or visit their web site at www.womenlobby.org

© *European Women's Lobby*

Where have all the women gone?

They still earn less than their male counterparts and only one in 10 company directors are female. Why are women still struggling to achieve equality at work, asks Dolly Dhingra

How equal is 21st-century woman in the workplace? When it comes to management, 30% of managers are women yet they earn considerably less than their male counterparts – 24% less per hour, according to new figures from the Equal Opportunities Commission.

There has been significant progress – since the mid-1990s the number of female executives has doubled and the number of female company directors has tripled. Despite these increases only one in 10 company directors are women.

The EOC's report into British management reveals that female managers are more concentrated in certain careers, and clusters continue in particular industries. There are plenty of them in personnel, training and industrial relations, yet there are fewer than one in five IT managers. In some industries, they remain non-existent at certain levels – for example, there are no female chief constables. A higher proportion of women managers work in the public sector than in the private sector and they constitute two-thirds of managers in health and social work – and just 10% in construction.

The findings are not a huge surprise, says EOC chairwoman Julie Mellor. 'They confirm our suspicions that women simply aren't represented at senior level in many industries. What is particularly disappointing is how big the impact of raising children is on women's careers. Female managers are much less likely to have dependent children than their male colleagues.'

The EOC remains concerned about Britain's 'glass ceiling' where senior positions are still mysteriously elusive to women in some industries. The report says: 'The EOC would like to see employers opening non-traditional opportunities through staff development and improved recruitment practices.'

The EOC remains concerned about Britain's 'glass ceiling' where senior positions are still mysteriously elusive to women in some industries

---

Sarah Best, senior policy adviser at the Confederation of British Industry, suggests a few ideas that these companies might implement. 'We could learn a thing or two from the US and adopt best practice such as mentoring, networking and career tracking schemes.' Male-dominated industries could also do with an image makeover, she says. 'Employers have actively to change the image of their companies and this has to work its way down to universities, colleges and schools. Careers advisers in schools have to be more imaginative and ensure females aren't just channelled into the traditional stereotypical industries such as social services.' She also believes the state should provide childcare.

Behavioural expert and corporate trainer Judi James says the reason women are highly represented in certain industries is not due to any gender-specific psychology. 'It's a really iffy stereotype to think women prefer the caring professions. The problem is that the doors of opportunity are far more visible and open in those industries and this is not necessarily the case in the private sector or in male-dominated industries.'

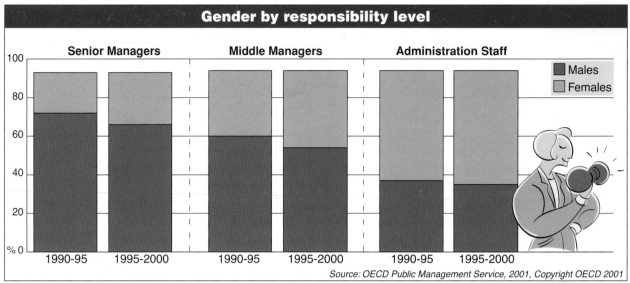

Gender by responsibility level

	Senior Managers		Middle Managers		Administration Staff	
	1990-95	1995-2000	1990-95	1995-2000	1990-95	1995-2000

Males
Females

Source: OECD Public Management Service, 2001, Copyright OECD 2001

James has been working with large numbers of female graduates who are choosing to work in the financial sector. 'At the moment, more women than men are moving into accountancy, but I don't know what happens to them after that. When I see people being groomed for partnership level, I don't see many women.'

The government also believes that career attitudes of men and women are creating pay differentials. Women have traditionally seen certain highly paid sectors of the economy as unattractive. Speaking at a recent conference on women in IT, Trade and Industry secretary Patricia Hewitt said: 'The current situation is bad for women. It means they are missing out on opportunities to earn the higher wages available in the IT sector. It's also bad for business and bad for the economy.'

The government's strategy is to encourage more women to take up careers in science, engineering and technology (SET). Free IT software is being supplied by US software company Macromedia to schools running computer clubs. Am-

bassadors of SET are to visit schools to encourage girls in particular to choose the subjects as long-term careers, and IT Compass – a free online advice service for women – is soon to be launched. Up to £1m is also being made available for the IT sector from the DTI's Work Life Balance Challenge Fund. This provides consultancy support for employees wanting to introduce innovative working practices.

'An IT industry dominated by men is using only half the available talent and creativity. That is a particular cause for concern in an industry that, despite current economic conditions, has a growing demand for skilled labour,' said Hewitt.

The EOC report makes recommendations to improve equality in the underrepresented industries. It suggests promoting part-time work and flexible working, and says employers have a duty to discourage the long-hours culture. James goes as far as to suggest that women may not be visible in these industries through choice.

'I think women may be more ahead of the game than many think,' she says. 'Some of these senior jobs such as company directors aren't up to much. A lot of people are missing out on having an enjoyable life. I'd like to know what these jobs have to offer that's so great? OK, you've got power but often what you can do is dictated by shareholders, the working environment is solitary, and if you make loads of money you don't have the time to enjoy it.'

'Women have to look at other ways of getting there. It may mean moving sideways for a while or leapfrogging through certain jobs'

If women choose not to take certain senior managerial positions, that is an individual matter. But if a glass ceiling is suspected, what can they do to break through it? If there is resistance to progression, then women may have to think creatively – the climb up the ladder may not be linear, says James. 'Women have to look at other ways of getting there. It may mean moving sideways for a while or leapfrogging through certain jobs.'

Executive coach Ian McDermott says that it may be a case of 'managing upwards'. It is often senior staff who generate obstacles at work, he says. 'Start to think of those above you as customers or clients. You need to make them perceive you as someone who makes their life easier, who can supply otherwise unavailable skills and information. Maintain a good rapport with them and make it clear that you are supporting them rather than acting as a threat.'

• For more information about the EOC, log on to www.eoc.org.uk, and for the SET initiative, visit www.set4women.gov.uk

Give us a job!

Does sex make a difference?

In the last 50 years, the UK labour market has changed dramatically. Gone are the days when men went out to work and women stayed at home to look after the children. Today women make up nearly half the workforce, and projections show that in 10 years' time they will fill most of the two million extra jobs on offer.

But although more and more women are returning to work after childbirth, it is still overwhelmingly women who are responsible for looking after the children or arranging childcare facilities. They spend twice as much time as men on cleaning and six times as much on washing and ironing clothes. Not surprisingly, far more women than men work part time and flexible hours.

Key facts

There are around 17.5 million women of working age in the UK, compared to 18.6 million men.

- Women are less likely than men to be in employment – 70% of all working-age women are in work, compared with 80% of all working-age men
- Minority ethnic women are less likely to be employed than white women
- The employment rate for women with children is lower than those without – fewer than 50% of working-age women with a child aged under two are in employment
- Of those in employment, more than two-fifths (43%) of women work part time

Women are less likely than men to be in employment – 70% of all working-age women are in work, compared with 80% of all working-age men

- Women are less likely than men to be self-employed – 6.5% of women compared to 15% of men
- Although women still only account for one-third of new business start-ups, the rate of female self-employment has more than doubled over the last 20 years
- Women graduates as young as 20 can expect to be paid 15% less than men
- On average girls get less pocket money – 63p for boys for laying the table, but only 50p for girls; £2 for boys taking the rubbish out but only 59p for girls
- Women make up just 24% of managers and just under 10% of directors in companies
- Of the top 100 companies listed on the stock exchange (FTSE 100), only one has a woman heading it

Do boys do different jobs from girls?

Although women make up half the labour force, they are often still stereotyped into a narrow range of jobs – as secretaries, nurses, cooks and cleaners.

For instance, 90% of the students who took a health and social care vocational qualification in 2001 were female; 81% of those taking IT were male. Similar 'segregation' occurs in the workplace. About 96% of people taking engineering apprenticeships are men, whereas 89% of health and social care apprentices are women.

Does it matter if boys do different jobs from girls?

It is important that both boys and girls have the opportunity to fulfil their potential, based on their talents and interests rather than their gender. Girls should be offered the same opportunities as boys to pursue whatever career most interests them – whether it is science, engineering and IT or

social care, nursing and hairdressing, or even the chance to set up their own business.

These decisions – being made as early as year 9 – will have a long-term impact on the earnings potential of boys and girls. One of the reasons for the pay gap is because of occupational segregation.

Women in information technology (IT)

The IT industry is currently facing a skills shortage in a number of areas – it is keen to recruit qualified engineers, technicians and software developers.

Despite that, the number of women working in the industry is falling – recent statistics show that women make up less than a third of employees in the whole IT sector. When you look at specific jobs involving the development and production of technology, the figure drops still further.

Key facts

In 1997, women made up 27% of those working in the IT sector. By 2002 that figure had dropped to 23%.

- Within the sector, women make up 27% of database assistants and clerks, but only 7% of IT strategy and planning professionals
- Women make up only a fifth of computing graduates in the UK
- The percentage of women engineering graduates in the UK is 15%
- The percentage of women graduates in architecture, building and planning is 27%

- In 2001, about 4,000 girls got an A-Level in computer science, compared to just over 13,000 boys (a success rate of 87% for girls and 83% for boys)

Why are girls not interested in IT jobs?

In the UK, girls tend to disengage from IT subjects between the ages of 11 and 15. Because so many IT jobs are done by men and seem very 'techy', the sector has acquired a masculine image. If it is to encourage more women into IT careers, it needs to shake off this image.

How do we make sure girls are more attracted to IT jobs?

There are a number of initiatives that can be introduced to try to counteract the lack of 'psychological' access to IT by women. For instance:
- Developing IT capabilities among teachers (particularly women teachers)
- Creating specific opportunities for girls to get involved with technology at school, such as all-girl computer clubs
- Making sure that teaching resources are relevant to both girls and boys
- Thinking about the way that courses are branded and marketed – for instance a course in computing will not attract many women, but a course in business and IT will attract equal numbers of men and women
- Improving the working practices and business culture in IT workplaces
- Improving access for women with child care responsibilities

Women in science, engineering and technology (SET)

Scientists, engineers and technologists make a huge contribution to the UK's economy, from working

---

Women graduates as young as 20 can expect to be paid 15% less than men

---

in the health service to protecting the environment. Their scientific and engineering skills underpin the UK's research and development, and thereby our innovation performance.

Women are under-represented in most science subjects, both at undergraduate and postgraduate level. And where they have taken those degrees, too often they get stuck at the bottom of the career ladder. For minority ethnic women, the problem is even more acute.

Key facts
- In 1984, only 7% of engineering graduates were women, but by 2000 it was 15%
- In 2000, less than 3% of chartered engineers were women
- Although girls outperform boys at GCSE science, it is only by 1% in physics compared to 15% in English
- Between 1995 and 2000, the number of boys awarded with an A level in physics fell by 1.6%; the number of girls rose by 8.7%
- Three times more boys than girls were awarded a physics A Level in 2000

How many girls study science?

The number of girls taking SET subjects – particularly physics, computer science and engineering – is low. Although lots of girls take biology, far fewer take A-level physics. Over twice as many boys take maths and science-based vocational qualifications. The gender divide is even bigger for modern apprenticeships.

Although there are valid concerns about the under-achievement of boys at school, there are also plenty of reasons to be concerned about the lack of girls taking SET subjects. That's why girls, in particular, need to be informed of their choices prior to GCSE, when many of them rule out science as a possible career choice. Schools have a significant role to play in this.

What motivates girls?

Recent research has shown that more girls than boys are interested in socially relevant work. And they want a job that involves teamwork and offers security. The trouble is that too many of them think that a career in SET will not give them any of that.

On top of that, girls see science as dull and boring and a scientist as a clever middle-aged man working alone in a laboratory – perceptions that discourage them from SET careers. If more girls are to become engineers, nuclear physicists or computer programmers, they need a more positive image of the industry than this one.

- The above information is an extract from *Does sex make a difference? – An equalities pack for young people on International Women's Day*, February 2003, published by the DTI's Women and Equality Unit.
© Crown copyright

Women directors come out on top

Information from the Chartered Management Institute

Women directors received higher salary increases than their male counterparts, according to the 2002 National Management Salary Survey, launched earlier this year by the Chartered Management Institute and Remuneration Economics. The survey, which compares salaries and total earnings for men and women managers at all levels, showed average salary increases for female directors of 9.3 per cent over the last year, against only 5.6 per cent increases for male directors.

Women managers also received higher salary increases than their male colleagues, averaging 6.5 per cent increases against male increases of just 6.1 per cent.

Possible reasons for this disparity could be that stock market turbulence over the last year has had a knock-on effect on private sector salaries. With women making up only two per cent of FTSE company executive directors, market uncertainty will have had much less effect on their salaries. Also, the public sector has benefited over this period from increased investment, which is beginning to address the disparity in pay levels between the sectors.

Numbers of female managers

The number of women directors has also jumped from one in ten (9.9 per cent) to one in seven (14.8 per cent) this year according to the survey, which confirms that the majority of women directors are employed in Public Sector or in Finance and Business Services.

The number of female managers as a percentage of the total workforce, as measured by the sample, has risen to 30 per cent – more than double the figure recorded six years ago.

The increase over the past decade, as shown by the table on this

inspiring leaders

page, can be attributed to more women entering higher education and the growth in the number of couples who are both working. Another reason may well be the decline in the manufacturing sector and rise of service industries, where the qualities of management most often attributed to women are also those associated with the skills needed to succeed in customer-focused and service-oriented organisations.

Those industries reflecting the greatest percentage of women managers (more than 30 per cent) are the public sector, finance and business and the chemicals industry.

By function, women are most represented in HR and insurance, where they make up more than 50 per cent of managers overall, and least represented in manufacturing and production, where they make up only around 6 per cent of managers.

Comparative rates of pay

At nearly every level of management, women are still earning less than their male equivalents, though the gap is narrowing as their salaries increase faster. The lowest levels of management still show the widest discrepancy of pay between men and women.

Reasons for this continuing discrepancy may include the fact that, according to this survey, women managers are more likely to achieve senior positions within the public sector, where annual bonuses are not normally paid. Despite the fact that salary levels are increasing more for women, private sector bonuses may still be inflating the total earnings figures for male managers.

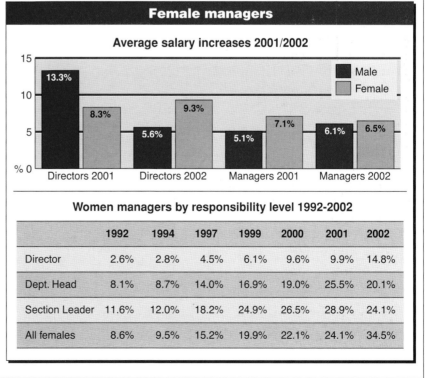

Female managers

Average salary increases 2001/2002

- Directors 2001: Male 13.3%, Female 8.3%
- Directors 2002: Male 5.6%, Female 9.3%
- Managers 2001: Male 5.1%, Female 7.1%
- Managers 2002: Male 6.1%, Female 6.5%

Women managers by responsibility level 1992-2002

	1992	1994	1997	1999	2000	2001	2002
Director	2.6%	2.8%	4.5%	6.1%	9.6%	9.9%	14.8%
Dept. Head	8.1%	8.7%	14.0%	16.9%	19.0%	25.5%	20.1%
Section Leader	11.6%	12.0%	18.2%	24.9%	26.5%	28.9%	24.1%
All females	8.6%	9.5%	15.2%	19.9%	22.1%	24.1%	34.5%

Mary Chapman, Chief Executive of the Chartered Management Institute, said of the findings: 'It is encouraging to see, for the first time this year, that salary increases are higher for women managers than for men. This should go some way to reducing the continuing discrepancies in total earnings. At lower levels of management in particular, women are consistently paid less than their male counterparts.'

Women in management – fast facts

- In 2000/2001 there were 1,210,000 female managers/senior officials in the UK compared with 2,726,000 men.
- 80 per cent of women in senior management positions believe that commitment to family responsibilities hinders their advancement in the workplace.
- Reasons for the pay gap are complex and interconnected. The key factors are thought to be: human capital differences; part-time working; travel patterns; occupational segregation and workplace segregation. Other factors that affect the gender pay gap include: job practices, appraisal systems, reward systems and retention measures, wage-setting practices and discrimination.
- 72 per cent of working-age women are economically active.
- 41 per cent of women who are married or living with a partner are the main breadwinners, and 33 per cent earn the same as their partner.
- 60 per cent of married or cohabiting mothers with children under five work. This rises to 70 per cent of those with children under 10.
- 30 per cent of all women work part-time.

'It is encouraging to see, for the first time this year, that salary increases are higher for women managers than for men'

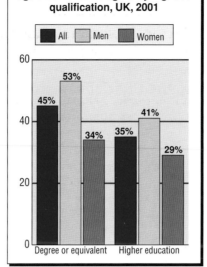

Qualification

Proportion of employees of working age that were managers by highest qualification, UK, 2001

Legend: ■ All □ Men ▦ Women

Degree or equivalent: All 45%, Men 53%, Women 34%
Higher education: All 35%, Men 41%, Women 29%

- As the champion of management, the Chartered Management Institute shapes and supports the managers of tomorrow, helping them deliver results in a dynamic world. The Institute helps set and raise standards in management, encouraging development to improve performance. Moreover, with in-depth research and regular policy surveys of its 91,000 individual members and 520 corporate members, the Institute has a deep understanding of the key issues.

- The above information is from the Chartered Management Institute's web site which can be found at www.managers.org.uk

© *Chartered Management Institute*

Women march slowly to the top

The number of women executive directors among Britain's top firms has risen by 50 per cent in the last year. But even with this increase, women still make up just 3 per cent of executive directors in the FTSE top 100 firms.

And while most of the companies have female directors on their boards, women represent just 7 per cent of total board members.

The 2002 Female FTSE Report, published yesterday, shows that 84 of the 1,161 directors of high-ranking companies are women.

Of those, 15 are executive directors who have a daily role in the running of the business.

This is five more than last year and the number is rising for the first time in four years.

Marks and Spencer topped the list for the second year running with women making up 27 per cent of their 11-member board. Sainsbury's jumped 25 places to come in just below M&S with 25 per cent women.

Airport company BAA and chemical firm AstraZeneca earned joint third place with 23 per cent female membership.

But 39 of the top 100 firms have all-male boards, including ICI, British American Tobacco and Rolls Royce.

Speaking at the Women's Leadership Summit, which coincided with the launch of the report, Solicitor General Harriet Harman said yesterday: 'The situation is not good and we really need to make better progress.

'The companies who have no females on their board seem to think women have nothing to say at that level in the company.'

She added: 'There should be no companies with all-male boards.'

Among the 100 companies there was one female chief executive, Marjorie Scardino of Pearson, and one woman chairman, Baroness Hogg of 3i.

The survey also found that female board members were six years younger than their male counterparts on average, and that nearly half the women directors were appointed in the last three years.

© *The Daily Mail*
November, 2002

The fight for equal pay

Now the boss must tell women workers what he pays men. New law aimed at helping females fight for equal pay

Women are to be given the right to know how much male colleagues are being paid for doing the same job.

Under new employment laws they will be able to find out confidential details by submitting a simple questionnaire to the boss.

The Government says the controversial measure will help women fight for equal pay – studies show they are paid an average of 18 per cent less than men for the same work.

But employers warned yesterday that the move would ignite bad feeling and rows between staff and could lead to a surge in litigation.

Ruth Lea, head of policy at the Institute of Directors, said: 'How much you earn is something people regard as very confidential. I wouldn't want anyone to know what my salary is and I don't suppose my colleagues would. I think this could lead to a lot of upset in the workplace.

'It's all the more scope for people to go to tribunals. I think we could see more legal action.'

The issue of equal pay has been highlighted by a string of high-profile battles.

Investment banker Julie Bower successfully challenged Schroder Securities after being paid a £25,000 bonus while two male colleagues received £1.1 million between them. The new measure will come into effect in April 2003. The questionnaire will set out a complainant's grievance and ask for specific information from the employer, particularly about named employees.

Women will be able to use the answers as ammunition in an unfair pay case.

The male colleagues involved will be able to veto salary disclosure, and employers will also be able to refuse to comply with the request.

But such a refusal would be likely to trigger legal action and would count against the firm at an employment tribunal.

By Jo Butler, Home Affairs Correspondent

The Department of Trade and Industry said it was hoped that once a discrepancy had been revealed, employers would raise the pay of the woman rather than fight it out in the courts.

A spokesman said that the threat of women using the questionnaires should encourage bosses to think twice before paying men more.

Employment lawyers have warned firms to consider the implications of the new rules when they set annual bonuses in the next few weeks.

> *The threat of women using the questionnaires should encourage bosses to think twice before paying men more*

The awards, traditionally paid at Christmas, could come under scrutiny when the new regulations take effect.

Any discrepancies between handouts to men and women could leave firms vulnerable to action.

EQUAL PAY NOW!

The Equal Opportunities Commission said it expected a lot of women to seize on the new right, which would be a powerful weapon in the fight for equal pay.

It said that a survey had found that 77 per cent of people had never asked their colleagues what they earned and a quarter had no idea what workmates took home.

But the EOC admitted the idea raised a lot of issues about confidentiality of information.

It is understood staff could use the law only to discover the salary of colleagues on a similar pay scale or professional level at a company. It would not let secretaries find out the wages of the chief executive, for example.

Men will also be able to use the new right if they believe they are being paid less than women.

Susan Anderson, director of human resources policy at the Confederation of British Industry, said equal pay questionnaires would be welcome if they helped resolve disputes without having to go to court.

But she said: 'Firms need reassurance that this is to tackle genuine pay concerns, not a blank cheque for employees to find out what colleagues earn.'

The final format of the questionnaires, similar to those already used for suspected racial, sexual or disability discrimination, has yet to be decided.

The questionnaires are a key part of the new Employment Act brought in by Trade and Industry Secretary Patricia Hewitt this summer and designed to encourage 'family friendly' working practices.

It also gives women more rights to maternity leave, introduces paternity leave and forces employers to consider requests for flexible working arrangements.

© The Daily Mail
December 2002

Equal pay

Information from the Fawcett Society

Why is the pay gap an important issue?

The pay gap is the difference in average earnings between men and women. It affects women throughout their lives and is found in all industries and occupations. If men and women had equal pay, it would make a significant contribution to ending child poverty, help women achieve their full potential and end the cycle of lifetime inequality that results in women's poverty in old age.

Facts and figures

- Women working full time earn 80% of the hourly rate of a man working full time.
  (*Women & Men in the UK: Women's Unit 2000*)
- Women working part time earn on average 58% of the hourly rate of a man working full time.
  (*Women & Men in the UK: Women's Unit 2000*)
- Britain's equal pay record is poor when compared to other European countries – tenth out of fifteen countries surveyed.
  (EOC *Valuing Women* 2000)
- Over a lifetime the gender pay gap can cost a childless mid skilled woman just under £250,000.[1]

Pay gap v. earnings gap

The difference between men and women's hourly earnings does not reveal the true extent of the differences in men and women's earnings.

- Women working full time earn only 72% of men's full-time average weekly earnings although they earn 80% of their hourly rate.

This is because on average men work longer hours than women.[2] Women are often less able to work long hours as they continue to shoulder more family/household responsibilities.

Traditionally male-dominated sectors are more likely to attract overtime or 'shift' payments. This adds to the disparity when earnings are looked at in a weekly rather than hourly time frame.

Having children does affect a mother's employment patterns. Nearly 50% of women whose youngest child is under 5 are not in employment and of those who do work, 65% work part time. Poorer pay is associated with part-time work.

- It is calculated that a mid skilled mother of two, loses an additional £140,000 of her potential earnings after childbirth.[3]

Ethnicity and pay

Ethnicity affects pay for both men and women. For all ethnic minority groups, men experience lower than average rates of hourly pay than white men, therefore the pay gap between men and women of minority ethnic groups appears much smaller. However, this hides important variations between different ethnic minorities.

- Pakistani and Bangladeshi women earn on average 84% of the average hourly rates of white women.[4]

What are the main causes of the pay gap between men and women?

1. Discrimination

Work by the LSE calculates that up to 42% of the gender pay gap is attributable to direct discrimination against women.[5] Since 1995 the number of equal pay cases registered with employment tribunals has more than doubled.[6]

Equal pay is not just about salaries and wages, it is also about the total package which employers offer their employees, this includes bonuses, overtime and pensions.

Case study

In January 2002 a city analyst, forced out of her job, won a case against an investment bank for unfair dismissal and sex discrimination after being awarded a bonus of £25,000 whilst male colleagues received £440,000 and £650,000.

2. Part-time work

Although the pay gap overall has declined, the pay of women working part time relative to men working full time has not.

- In 1998, women part-timers earned 59% of hourly earnings of a male full-timer, the same proportion as in 1978.
- In 1998, 44% of all women in employment in the UK worked part time.

Women make up the majority of part-time workers. Part-time work for women is often a long-term state rather than the stepping stone to full-time employment it is for men. There are also limited opportunities to work part time in higher grade occupations.

There is no objective reason why working part time should mean poorer pay.

Part-time workers' regulations (introduced July 2000) will go some way towards helping close the pay gap. Employers will not be able to pay a part-time worker less than a full-time worker doing the same job, simply because they are part time.

3. 'Women's' work

In 1995, 60% of all British women were employed within the ten most feminised occupations. Within these occupations the workforce was 80% female.[7] These occupations include sales assistant, domestics and cleaners, nurses, care assistants and teachers.

These highly feminised occupations have a higher than average share of part-time workers,[7] which often means poorer wages. Women working in feminised sectors experienced a higher than average wage shortfall.

- Women working part time in the 'top ten' feminised industries earned 57% of men's average pay.
- Women working full time in these sectors earned 78%.

Women working outside feminised occupations experienced a much smaller pay gap – 68% for part-timers and 92% for full-timers.[8]

Women in feminised occupations find that their work is given a lower status (translating into lower pay levels) than that of traditionally male occupations. This is due to the misconception that women's wages are not vital to household income and because many 'feminised' occupations are associated with caring which is still undervalued in our society.

The Equal Pay Act can help if women can prove that they are being paid less than a male colleague where the work is different but of equal value in terms of the demands of the job

---

Case Study

MSF won a landmark case on behalf of speech therapists who successfully claimed equal pay with clinical psychologists and pharmacists. The case, including back pay, could be worth £100 million.

In May 2000 in a deal worth £12 million, NHS speech therapists lifted the glass ceiling and extended their career ladder. Those who reach the top will have pay rates £12,000-15,000 higher than was possible under the old structure – putting the profession, whose recruits are mainly women, on a par with clinical psychologists and pharmacists, jobs which draw larger numbers of men.

Many women continue to work in these sectors because, despite the poorer pay, these occupations offer the flexibility that many women need in order to balance family and work responsibilities. In addition, stereotyping in education careers advice and of wider society all play a role in steering women towards occupations they have traditionally worked in.

---

4. Horizontal segregation

Women make up a smaller proportion of the workforce higher up the responsibility and pay ladder.

This is obvious in professions such as teaching and nursing where despite women making up the vast majority of entry levels to these professions, men are over-represented at senior and managerial levels.

- Women make up 54.4% of classroom teachers in secondary schools but only 27% of secondary head teachers are women.
- Only 11.7% of primary school classroom teachers are men, they make up 42.7% of primary head teachers.

What does the law say?

The Sex Discrimination Act (SDA) came into force in 1975.

The Equal Pay Act (EPA) took effect in 1975 and was amended in 1984.

- The SDA makes it unlawful to discriminate on the grounds of sex.
- Specifically sex discrimination is not allowed in employment, education, advertising or when providing housing, goods, services or facilities.
- Employers must not discriminate against an individual because of their sex or because they are married.
- This applies to recruitment, treatment in the job, chances for promotion and training, dismissal or redundancy.
- The EPA says women must be paid the same as men when they are doing the same job or work which has been rated as equivalent or of equal value.

Recent developments: Kingsmill Review

Key recommendations

- Mandatory reporting on women's employment and pay in Operational and Financial Reviews.
- Private and public sector organisations to be encouraged to conduct employment and pay reviews.
- Government to monitor progress with employment and pay reviews in the private sector with a view to considering the need for legislation at a future date.

The Equal Pay Act can help if women can prove that they are being paid less than a male colleague where the work is different but of equal value in terms of the demands of the job

---

- New academic centre for excellence to be established by Government to look at careers and labour market prospects for women.
- Overhaul of 'Investors in People' award to include women's employment and pay issues.
- Consideration of introduction of right for employees to request employer to confirm whether they are receiving remuneration equal to a named colleague.
- Tax credits for employers providing training for low-paid employees and those who recruit and train women in under-represented industries

The Government have agreed to carry out pay reviews of their own departments and agencies by 2003.

New Initiatives also include:

The Castle Awards: recognising employer excellence in addressing equal pay.

Fair Pay Champions: from business, unions and to raise the profile of the issue.

Burden of Proof Directive: (introduced October 2001) makes two technical changes to the Sex Discrimination Act 1975:

1. Changed the burden of proof. After applicants have established the facts, it is then up to the employer to show that there is a non-discriminatory reason for their actions.
2. Clarifies the meaning of indirect discrimination.

Equal pay taskforce

An independent taskforce set up by the EOC and business led, considered how to eliminate discrimination in pay systems. Its report (February 2001) recommended:
- publicising the facts
- improving equal pay legislation, introducing mandatory pay re-

The Equal Pay Task Force concluded that it would be feasible, for the gender pay gap to be eliminated entirely within 8 years

views and a streamlined tribunal process
- improved guidance for employers and unions and a Government requirement for pay reviews in the public sector
- opening up discussion about pay, reporting of pay reviews in employers' annual report
- the Government should use policies such as the National Minimum Wage, the National Childcare Strategy, and the National Skills agenda to help narrow the pay gap.

Where next?

Despite 30 years of equal pay legislation the pay gap between men and women has not closed.

The Equal Pay Task Force concluded that it would be feasible, for the gender pay gap to be eliminated entirely within 8 years.

Fawcett would like to see both the Sex Discrimination Act and the Equal Pay Act overhauled.

Legislation should be made more effective by:
- Raising awareness about unequal pay; the vast majority of employers do not believe they have a pay gap in their organisation which means they do not see the need to undertake pay reviews.
- Introducing a mandatory system of pay audits for employers which is workable and enforceable.
- Requiring companies to report on their pay audits.
- Overhauling the employment tribunal process. Currently cases can drag on for years, which is unfair for both the employee and employer.
- Giving Tribunals the power to make general findings – which would have a wider effect than

the current system where judgements only apply to individual cases.
- Tribunals should also be allowed to rule on the question of equal value, before proceeding with the case.
- Allowing unions or others to bring claims on behalf of workers.
- Making the concept of 'equal pay for work of equal value' more accessible would help women to achieve equal pay by allowing hypothetical comparators.
- The Government also has a vital role as an employer of women.

We would like to see the public sector leading the way to ensure best practice in terms of reviewing pay systems.

References

1 Women's Unit Research on *Women's Incomes over a Lifetime* (2000) use simulated models to generate a lifetime earnings profile for women and men.
2 In Spring 1998 7% of women worked more than 48 hours a week compared to 30% of men (*Women and Men in the UK Facts & Figures 2000*; Women's Unit).
3 Women's Unit Research on *Women's Incomes over a Lifetime* (2000) use simulated models to generate a lifetime earnings profile for women and men.
4 ONS Labour Force Survey using four-quarter average from Spring 1998 to Winter 1998-99, cited in *Women's Incomes over a Lifetime* (Women's Unit Research 2000). Figures based on small samples so should be treated with caution.
5 *Women's Pay – Is discrimination still an issue?*, Swaffield, Centre-Piece, Spring 2000.
6 EOC 'Pay and Income' 1999.
7 55% of those working in the top ten feminised occupations were working part time compared to an average of 44%.
8 All figures from *Women's Incomes over a Lifetime* Women's Unit 2000

- The above information is from a briefing produced by the Fawcett Society. See page 41 for their address details.

Understanding the gender pay gap

Information from the Women and Equality Unit

The Women and Equality Unit has published a new report *The Gender Pay Gap* which looks at the causes of the gender pay gap.

It finds that the reasons for the pay gap are complex and inter-connected. Key factors include:

- Human capital differences
- Part-time working
- Travel patterns
- Occupational segregation
- Workplace segregation

Human capital differences: i.e. differences in educational levels and work experience

Historical differences in the levels of qualifications held by men and women have contributed to the pay gap. However, women are still more likely than men to have breaks from paid work to care for children and other dependants. These breaks impact on women's level of work experience, which in turn impacts on their pay rates.

Women are still under-represented in the higher paid jobs within occupations – the 'glass ceiling' effect

---

Part-time working

The pay gap between women working part time and men working full time is particularly large and, as a large proportion of women work part time, this is a major contributor to the gender pay gap. Some of this gap is due to part-time workers having lower levels of qualifications and less work experience. However, it is also due to part-time work being concentrated in less well-paid occupations.

Travel patterns

On average, women spend less time commuting than men. This may be because of time constraints due to balancing work and caring responsibilities. This can impact on women's pay in two ways. They will have a smaller pool of jobs to choose from. It may also result in lots of women wanting work in the same location (i.e. near to where they live) which will result in lower wages for those jobs.

Occupational segregation

Women's employment is highly concentrated in certain occupations (60 per cent of working women work in just 10 occupations). And those occupations which are female-dominated are often the lowest paid occupations. In addition, women are still under-represented in the higher paid jobs within occupations – the 'glass ceiling' effect.

Workplace segregation

At the level of individual workplaces, high concentration of female employees are associated with relatively low rates of pay. And higher levels of part-time working are associated with lower rates of pay, even after other factors have been taken into account.

Other factors which affect the gender pay gap include: job grading practices, appraisal systems, reward systems and retention measures, wage-setting practices and discrimination.

- The above information is from the Government's Women and Equality Unit's web site which can be found at www.womenandequalityunit.gov.uk

© Crown copyright

Gender segregation by industrial sector

Women's employment is largely concentrated in services in private households, health, education and in other care-related activities as well as manufacture, transport, agriculture and financial services.

Percentage of the jobs in each sector that are occupied by men and women in employment

NACE sectors[1]	Men all	Women all	Total
Construction	91%	9%	100%
Extraction	84%	16%	100%
Utilities	84%	16%	100%
Transport and communications	75%	25%	100%
Manufacturing	73%	27%	100%
Agriculture	66%	34%	100%
Financial services	58%	42%	100%
Public administration	56%	44%	100%
Sales, hotels and catering	47%	53%	100%
Other community services	44%	56%	100%
Health education	25%	75%	100%
Private households and extra-territorial	5%	95%	100%
All employment	56%	44%	100%

1 Sectors are ranked by the degree of male-dominated segregation.

Source: Third European Working Conditions Survey 2000

Rising trend in inequality

Rising trend in inequality revealed as more earn below the average

Nearly two-thirds of full-time employees now receive less than the average gross weekly earnings of £465. Since 1990, pay rises for the top earners have continued to outstrip those for the rest of the workforce to such an extent that the average wage has been pulled upwards, leaving more and more employees earning beneath it. The chart below shows the number of below-average earners rising from 61.2 per cent in 1990 to 64.6 per cent in 2002. The strongest rise has been in the years since 1997.

In the last ten years, the top earnings decile (the level above which 10 per cent of employees earn) has risen by 53.7 per cent, while the lowest earnings decile has grown by just 45.6 per cent. Employees at the highest decile earned £752.4 a week in 2002, 3.49 times the income of those at the lowest decile, who earned £215.6 a week.

The gap between the top and bottom earnings decile has widened at a faster pace for male employees than for female employees

---

Impact of NMW

Since the National Minimum Wage took effect in 1999, the bottom earnings decile has grown at a faster rate than in the rest of the 1990s when it was falling behind. It has clearly had a beneficial effect at the bottom of the earnings distribution. Between April 1999 and April 2002, the NMW rose by 13.8 per cent and the bottom decile of earnings increased by 13.3 per cent. However, earnings at the lower quartile, and to a lesser extent at the median, have grown at a slower rate in the post-NMW period.

The NMW has taken many very low earners over an income threshold and led to a greater concentration of people earning at levels just above it, but it has had little impact on overall inequality. This is because earnings at the upper quartile and particularly at the top decile, have continued to grow at a much faster pace, outstripping the gains made by those at the bottom.

The gap between the top and bottom 10 per cent for all employees grew considerably throughout the 1980s, it then continued to widen but at a slower pace through the recession of the early 1990s, with an acceleration in the widening during the recovery between 1994 and 1995.

Top male earners widen inequality

The gap between the top and bottom earnings decile has widened at a faster pace for male employees than for female employees. This is the result of higher earnings growth for the most highly-paid men, such as finance professionals and senior managers working in the City. The gains made by the top 5 per cent of male earners in 2002 were great enough to increase the average earnings level for all men by 0.7 per cent. This led to a widening of the gender pay gap, despite women's earnings growing at a faster rate than men's in the bottom 95 per cent of the workforce.

■ The above information is an extract from *Incomes Data Services Report* 874, February 2003.
© *Incomes Data Services (IDS)*

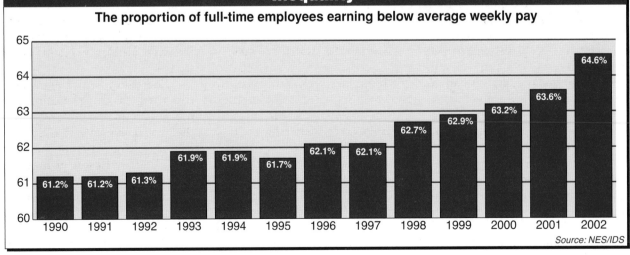

Inequality

The proportion of full-time employees earning below average weekly pay

Year	Value
1990	61.2%
1991	61.2%
1992	61.3%
1993	61.9%
1994	61.9%
1995	61.7%
1996	62.1%
1997	62.1%
1998	62.7%
1999	62.9%
2000	63.2%
2001	63.6%
2002	64.6%

Source: NES/IDS

Women struggle to join £100k club

Number of earners in the top pay bracket rises by 50% but the glass ceiling remains firmly in place

By Richard Wray

The number of people in Britain earning six-figure sums has increased by almost 50% in the past four years, though for women in business the glass ceiling is still very much in evidence.

Despite government efforts to get more of them into high-paying jobs, women are still a rarity among senior management and are being outpaced by their male counterparts when it comes to grabbing £100,000 or more.

The percentage of women in the top rank of wage-earners has hardly moved in the past four years, according to figures from the inland revenue. This year an estimated 326,000 people in this country will earn more than £100,000 of whom 41,000 – or 12% – are expected to be female. Four years ago there were 222,000 people getting six-figure pay packets but again 12% or 27,000 were women.

Denise Kingsmill, drafted in by the government to report on the gap between the salaries of men and women last year, believes Britain is losing out by not promoting women into the premier league. 'It's a huge cause for concern, it points to a waste of a national resource. Women are outperforming men at every academic level but if they are not reaching the top of organisations, as these figures suggest, this is a national scandal and a huge waste of the investment in women's education over the last 20 to 30 years.'

Britain's top earners are to be found in City jobs and senior management positions predominantly in the south-east.

In the male-dominated world of the City, women such as fund manager Nicola Horlick and Carol Galley, former joint head of Merrill Lynch Investment Managers, make the headlines mainly because of their rarity rather than their business acumen.

Women are even rarer at the top of British businesses. Marjorie Scardino, the chief executive of Pearson, owner of Penguin and the *Financial Times*, recently topped a *Management Today* table of Britain's 50 most powerful women, but she sits alone as the only female boss of one of Britain's top 100 publicly quoted companies. Baroness Hogg is one of the few women to have made it to the post of chairman of a FTSE 100 company, investment group 3i.

A report last year by Cranfield University's school of management found that the number of female directors involved in running British business had actually been falling over the past three years.

Among the companies listed on the London stock exchange only 57% had any female representation on their board last year, compared with 64% in 1999. When women do get a place at the boardroom table it tends to be as a part-time non-executive director.

Denise Kingsmill believes that British business is engaging in tokenism. 'There is still a tendency to think if you have one woman on the board then you do not need any more,' she says. 'This is holding back British business. It means companies are not focusing on getting the best people.'

Other experts believe that the lack of women among high earners owes much to Britain's working culture. 'Women tend to take on more caring responsibilities and find that they cannot progress in their careers at the same pace as men once they have had a career break,' said a spokesperson for the equal opportunities commission. 'There is still this misconception that you can only reach the top by buying into traditional working culture which demands excessive hours. This culture means that businesses lose out as they are denied women's talents and skills at senior decision-making levels.'

In March the EOC published research showing that as men and women progressed through their careers the pay gap widened. By the age of 35 women earn a third less than their male colleagues.

For some women in the City, taking a lower salary means getting a better style of life. Ruth Lea, head of policy at the Institute of Directors, spent six years in the City working for Japanese and American banks. She is in no doubt that many women place other priorities above earning bumper salaries, especially as they get older. 'I left the City and took a drop in salary – it was career choice for me, it was not that I felt I had been discriminated against,' she said.

'A friend recently told me that if I went back I could earn five or six times my salary and for half a millisecond I thought "hmmm perhaps", but I could not do it again. I have decided I would rather enjoy my life.'

She believes that arguments which suggest that the country is missing out on a tangible return on the investment made in education miss the point. 'Why do we have to look at education in terms of financial returns? To have a very educated woman who, for example, is looking after children is a return and a half.'

Thin on top!

Why men earn more and get promoted faster. The Work Foundation analysis of gender pay gap says employers often use previous salary history to pay women less

The Work Foundation urges employers to consider how they use job applicants' previous pay details when negotiating terms and conditions. In a report published in December 2001 the campaigning body says that employers often use previous salary history to pay women less – perpetuating the gender pay gap.

Small step or giant leap? Towards gender equality at work says that equal opportunities in the workplace has stalled and the Government should be prepared to make gender audits compulsory if employers remain indifferent to the pay gap.

Are men becoming the second sex?

The report rejects suggestions that men are becoming the second sex. It identifies the link between the pay gap and women's difficulty in getting higher status, better paid directorships or senior management positions. In 2002 only 15 women were executive directors in FTSE 100 companies and women are clustered at the lowest levels of management.

'Having women in those jobs would help reduce the difference between male and female earnings. But while top level positions remain largely two person careers – defined by long hours and high workloads, regular travel and even relocation, and assuming domestic support, typically by a wife – they will carry on being less accessible to women,' says Alexandra Jones, policy specialist. 'If we are serious about removing the pay gap, we must address the shortage of women at the top of British firms.'

Big wallets and small purses

According to the report, the pay gap also exists because male employees benefit from work cultures, job structures and the traditional career structure. Employers often rely on previous salary data as an indication

the work foundation

of an individual's market worth when making an offer. For women, whose, existing salary is likely to be much lower than a male counterpart, the use of salary history by employers often serves to keep them lower down the pay scales in comparison with men.

A US survey revealed that a large minority of people still believe staying at home to look after the children should be the mother's role. Only 1% felt fathers should stay at home.

Firms reward toughness, competitiveness and aggressiveness – qualities seen as masculine. Networks – important for making contacts and doing deals – consist mainly of men and are dominated by their interests and cultures.

Jobs offering flexibility and a local workplace often offer lower pay, because they are in high demand from women with children. Even highly skilled, female-dominated jobs such as nursing tend to pay less, because the skills and qualities needed are seen as 'natural' to women.

Responsibility for money is more highly rated and paid than responsibility for people – seen as a more feminine activity. And whereas women are valued on their performance, men are valued on their potential.

30 years of failed initiatives

The report outlines almost 30 years of initiatives which have failed to have a significant impact on the status quo:

'Fix the women' strategies – such as mentoring, skills training, 'bring your daughter to work' days or assertiveness courses. These address women's supposed weaknesses and leave the organisation and the labour market untouched.

'Add women and stir' – equal opportunities programmes which aim to remove the barriers that prevent women and other groups from entering male-dominated areas, and assume that more women at the top will make it easier for other women. Evidence shows that the majority of companies do the minimum and rarely encourage progressive equal opportunities. Furthermore many women who reach the top of organisations are unlikely or unwilling to 'rock the boat' by challenging the culture.

Managing diversity won support in the conservative backlash against political correctness and radical equal opportunities. It emphasises the business case which may mean that market needs override equality issues, and its focus on valuing people for their differences can also reinforce stereotypes.

Alexandra Jones says: 'The way we view, discuss and analyse inequality in the workplace is out of date and apologetic. If we really want to remove the barriers to women in the workplace, one of the first things we have to do is stop tinkering with a worn-out engine.'

The Work Foundation recommends:

- Supporting the move towards a single equality commission – which *Small Step Giant Leap* recommended in 2001. However, it is crucial that this is underpinned by a single equality act to ensure that one form of discrimination is not prioritised above another.
- Companies publishing strategies and information on equal pay in their annual reports. This should be seen as integral to diversity and CSR policies.

- An accreditation scheme for equality training. Run by the Equal Opportunities Commission, Commission for Racial Equality and Disability Rights Commission, this would be a quality check for the under-regulated equality training industry.
- Compulsory equality audits if progress on equal opportunities remains static.
- Specialist advisers on gender equality for SMEs.

- Employers providing more flexibility at all level in terms of working time, place and employment contracts. The introduction of the right to request flexible working for parents with children under 6 years old, part of employment legislation coming into force on April 6 2003, it is a positive start but more needs to be done to tackle the work cultures that value presenteeism and long hours working.

- Recognition of the important skills gained through running a home, as well as other caring roles and working in the community. Application forms and job interviews should reflect this.
- Making more use of collective bargaining to tackle the pay gap. Increased union membership among women could make collective bargaining more useful in promoting equal pay.

© The Work Foundation 2003

Winning equal pay

Equal pay developments in the UK

Equal pay legislation has been in force in the UK for over 30 years. Despite this, women's pay still lags behind that of men. The Government has made the closing of the gender pay gap a priority. Trade unions and employers are increasingly working in partnership to identify and eliminate pay discrimination. The achievement of equal pay for work of equal value is essential not only as a matter of social justice, but also for sound business reasons.

This briefing gives an outline of the extent of the pay gap, the findings of recent research, and identifies ways in which trade unions and employers can work together to achieve the goal of equal pay for work of equal value.

The pay gap

Despite 30 years of equal pay legislation,
- Women working full time still earn just 82p for every pound of the earnings of a full-time man. That's an 18% pay gap.
- For part-time workers the gap is even wider. And the gap for part-time workers has actually increased over the past two years. The hourly pay of women working part time is just 59% of the hourly earnings of men working full time.
- The pay gap is narrower where trade unions are recognised for pay bargaining.

- 24% of women compared to just 10% of men working full time earn less than £220 per week.
- Research by the Cabinet Office Women's Unit estimates that this female forfeit costs women with GCSEs over £241,000 of lost earnings over a lifetime.
- The research also identifies the mother gap which shows that mothers have an extra forfeit of £140,000 lost over a lifetime. And this forfeit increases with the number of children.
- The higher the level of education women attain, the narrower the gender pay gap. However, recent

research by the Equal Opportunities Commission shows that the starting salary for women graduates lags behind that of male graduates, even where they have studied similar subjects and gone into similar occupations. This graduate pay gap is estimated at 15%.

Causes of the pay gap

In October 1999 the Equal Opportunities Commission set up an Equal Pay Task Force to explore the issues of pay discrimination, take evidence and make recommendations about how to close the gap. The 12-member independent Task Force included senior figures from the private and the public sectors, from employers and trade unions, as well as experts in pay equality and gender issues. Over the year, the Task Force took evidence from a wide range of individuals and organisations, conducted a survey, commissioned research, held expert seminars and consulted key people.

The Task Force found three main factors contributing to the gender pay gap
- discrimination in pay
- occupational segregation
- the unequal impact of women's family responsibilities.

Occupational segregation
In the UK the labour market is highly segregated both vertically and horizontally.

- Horizontal segregation results in 60% of women working in just 10 occupational groups.
- Vertical segregation results in women being clustered in the lower grades of the occupations they work in.

Unequal impact of women's family responsibilities

Women still take the major responsibility for childcare. And an increasing number of women are also having to take responsibility for elder care. These responsibilities result in women having to take time out from work, not being able to meet the demands of the long-hours culture, having to work part time. All of which affect their earning power and opportunities for promotion.

Discrimination in pay systems

When all other factors and influences are taken into account the Task Force concluded that discrimination in pay systems accounts for between 25% and 50% of the pay gap. This is not only unacceptable on grounds of equity and social justice, but is also unlawful.

How does pay discrimination happen?

Many organisations and their workforce believe that because they have the same rate of pay for men and women, they have equal pay. However, over the years pay systems have developed and become more and more complex. Value judgements are often made about the pay points for individual employees. These can often discriminate against women. Recent equal pay cases have revealed discrimination in the application of pay systems relating to issues such as:
- Performance-related pay
- Bonus schemes
- Lack of transparency in pay systems.

This pay discrimination impacts on women by, for example:
- Giving them lower starting salaries than men.
- Women being excluded from bonus schemes.
- Women not qualifying for long-service awards.
- Women getting lower marks in performance monitoring.

Equal Pay Task Force recommendations

The Equal Pay Task Force made a number of recommendations for action by the social partners – government, employers and trade unions – to identify and tackle discrimination in pay systems. These are set out in detail in the report of the Task Force's work, *Just Pay*.

Key Task Force recommendations are to:
- Raise awareness of the issue
- Reform and modernise equal pay legislation
- Build the capacity of employers to achieve pay equity
- Enhance the transparency of pay systems.
- Amend social, economic and labour market policies.

Government response

In responding to the Task Force recommendations, the Government has introduced a number of initiatives to assist the social partners in efforts to close the pay gap. It is encouraging a voluntary approach by employers and trade unions, and has taken the following action:

Voluntary pay reviews

The Government has called on all employers to carry out voluntary pay reviews to identify any pay discrimination that exists and to develop policies to eliminate this pay gap.

It has provided the EOC with funding to produce a toolkit for use by employers to develop systems for reviewing pay. The EOC is also developing software for this.

Equal pay questionnaire

The Government has amended legislation to introduce the Equal Pay Questionnaire, similar to that used in sex discrimination cases. It is hoped this questionnaire will help to identify areas where pay inequality exists and assist in remedying this on a voluntary basis rather than needing to go to Tribunal.

Fair pay champions

The Government has appointed a number of fair pay champions to promote fair pay within the key sectors of the economy.

The Castle Awards

The Government has introduced the Castle Awards for those organisations who have taken action to eliminate pay discrimination and achieve equal pay.

Women working full time still earn just 82p for every pound of the earnings of a full-time man. That's an 18% pay gap

---

TUC training for equal pay representatives

The Government has provided funding for the Union Learning Fund to enable the TUC to train workplace equal pay representatives to enable them to work with employers in developing workplace pay reviews.

Reviewing pay systems

The EOC Code of Practice on Equal Pay makes a number of recommendations for employers on introducing an equal pay policy. Key points for such a policy would be to:

- Work in partnership with trade unions to develop the policy.
- Have a written equal pay policy with a clear statement of the organisation's commitment to achieve equal pay.
- Carry out pay reviews.
- Draw up an action plan to identify and eliminate pay discrimination.
- Build in systems for review and monitor the equal pay policy.
- Demonstrate commitment from the senior management down.

How pay reviews reveal pay inequalities

The Equal Pay Task Force report, *Just Pay*, provides a model for a preliminary stage in carrying out an equal pay review. Pay reviews have proved effective in revealing a number of factors which militate against pay equity, including:

Recruitment and promotion
- Women are often placed on a lower point on the pay scale at appointment or on promotion.
- Men have been found to bargain more on starting salaries.
- Long pay scales or ranges can mean it takes women a very long time to catch up.

Additional payments and benefits
Access to additional payments such as piece rates, bonuses and overtime are often unequal for men and women. In particular, in certain occupations such as sales, there may be a practice of awarding bonuses as a percentage of basic salaries. This may perpetuate the pay gap where men have a higher basic salary on which to measure their bonus.

It has often been the case that

Women are the overwhelming majority of part-time workers. Forty-three per cent of women, compared to eight per cent of men, work part time

---

typically men's jobs have been seen as likely to attract a bonus, whereas typically women's jobs have not. Such discrimination has been successfully challenged, for example in local government where school meals workers demonstrated that they should receive bonuses in the same way as caretakers.

Performance-related pay
The growth of performance-related pay has resulted in disparities within pay systems that have been shown to penalise not just women, but also disabled and black employees. Performance markings are frequently linked to appraisals.

Appraisal systems usually involve subjective value judgements about performance, and these may often be based on stereotyped assumptions. For example, judgements in discrimination cases have found that women and black workers have been disadvantaged when leadership skills are being assessed.

Indirect discrimination can also occur in appraisals, for example when rewarding long hours rather than objectively defined results.

Unequal treatment of part-time workers
Women are the overwhelming majority of part-time workers. Forty-three per cent of women, compared to eight per cent of men, work part time. The pay gap between the hourly pay of women working part time and men working full time has actually widened over the past year. Women working part time receive only 59p for every pound earned by male full-time workers. Continuing discrimination against part-time workers

---

is a major factor in perpetuating the gender pay gap. Despite the introduction, in the year 2000, of the Part Time Workers Regulations designed to achieve equal treatment for part-time workers, they are still disadvantaged in the workplace. Part-time workers are:

- even more likely than women in general to be concentrated in just a few occupations and in the lower grades in all the occupations
- often excluded from pay enhancements such as bonus payments, unsocial hours payments, weekend shift premia and bank holiday working premia
- less likely to have access to training and promotion opportunities.

Working together to close the gap

The time is right to work together to close the gender pay gap.
- The Government has made a commitment to tackle the gender pay gap
- The EOC has launched its Valuing Women campaign and is producing materials to assist employers and trade unions in achieving equal pay
- The trade unions have signalled their determination to close the gender pay gap and are investing in training for their representatives
- Employers are recognising the business case for achieving pay equity and having reward systems based on merit rather than prejudice.

Mind the gap? Yes we do!
Further information
UNISON web site: www.unison.org.uk/equalpay
EOC – Helpline 0845 601 5901 email: info@eoc.org.uk website: www.eoc.org.uk
Cabinet Office Women's & Equalities Unit – Tel: 020 7273 8828. Web site: www.womenandequalityunit.gov.uk

- The above information is from UNISON's Briefing on equal pay developments in UK. See page 41 for their address details.

© UNISON

Mind the gap!

Information from the Women and Equality Unit

Just over thirty years ago, the Equal Pay Act was introduced to stop pay discrimination between men and women. Since 1975 – when the law came into force – the pay gap has gone down from 30% to 19% today. For minority ethnic women, the problem is more acute, with Indian women facing a gap of nearly 27%.

What is the gender pay gap?

The pay gap is the average difference in earnings between men and women. That means that for every £1 that a man earns on average per hour, a woman earns £0.81 pence. This doesn't mean that a woman will always be paid less than a man, but the figures show that overall, women are paid almost a fifth less.

Key facts

- Women working full time earn 19% less per hour than men
- Women working part time earn 39% less per hour than men working full time
- Over the course of their working lives, women lose out to the tune of £250,000 just because they are women. If they have children, they stand to lose another £140,000
- The pay gap varies by age – from 2% for 16- to 19-year-olds to 34% for women over 50
- The pay gap is not unique to the UK – in the US, women earn an average of 72% of men's earnings; in Europe, women earn an average of 77%

Why is there a gender pay gap?

There are many reasons for the pay gap. It's not simply a question of men being paid more than women for doing the same job. Men and women have different work experiences, with women taking time out to have children. And women working part time find it harder to get the development opportunities they need to rise up their organisations.

Even travel patterns can have an impact on the pay gap. Government research has shown that women spend less time commuting than men, possibly because they want to be based near home. The knock-on effect, though, is that the job they take may be less well paid than one further away.

The following are some of the main reasons for the pay gap

- Occupational segregation, with too many women concentrated in a few occupations such as sales assistants, secretaries and cleaners. The figures show that 60% of women work in just 10 occupations.
- Caring responsibilities, resulting in many women taking breaks from their jobs to look after children or elderly dependants. These interruptions frequently mean that when women return to work, they take jobs that have a lower status (and pay) than when they took their break.
- Discrimination by employers paying women less than men although they are doing similar work. It is rare for an employer to deliberately pay a woman less. It usually comes about because of the grading system in place (with,

say, men doing technical jobs which have been traditionally better paid than cleaning or cooking), bonuses, availability of overtime, performance-related pay.

What can schools do about it?

Clearly, schools cannot directly tackle the pay gap. However, they can make sure that girls understand the long-term impact of the subject choices they make. Teachers and personal advisers can also encourage girls to take non-traditional subjects (such as information technology, science and engineering) by making these courses attractive and relevant to girls.

Connexions' personal advisers can give information, advice and practical help with all sorts of things like choosing subjects or mapping out future career options. This includes provision of advocacy and support mechanisms for young people considering non-traditional options.

- The above information is an extract from *Does sex make a difference? – An equalities pack for young people on International Women's Day*, February 2003, published by the DTI's Women and Equality Unit.
  © Crown copyright

Women in the armed forces

Information from the Ministry of Defence

Historical role of women in the UK armed forces

Women have played a vital role in the Armed Forces for many years. During the Second World War, for example, women were employed in a wide variety of roles, including many which exposed them to extreme danger. After the War, it was recognised that women continued to have an important role to play within the Armed Forces, and the Women's Services were permanently established. The early 1990s, however, saw the most dramatic peacetime changes in their duties, with women serving on surface ships, as aircrew for the first time, and in a much greater range of posts in the Army. Women's roles were also fully integrated and the separate Women's Services in the Army and Naval Service were abolished (the WRAF was never a separate Service, although the use of the term was discontinued).

Women in today's armed forces

These changes were taken a step further in 1998, and women today can be found in front-line appointments on ships, as pilots of combat aircraft, and a variety of roles in the Army including combat support roles in the Royal Artillery and Royal Engineers. They now take on many tasks that were once considered to be appropriate only to men and have done so with great success. In doing so, they make an

We are committed to ensuring that more and more women take advantage of the wide range of military careers open to them

Introduction

In 1997, the then Secretary of State for Defence announced that he was going to extend employment opportunities for women within the Armed Forces in line with their wider commitment to maximise the career opportunities for women. As a result, since 1998, women have been able to serve in 73% of posts in the Naval Service, 70% of posts in the Army, and 96% of posts in the RAF, and they now comprise more than 8% of the Armed Forces. Women continued to be excluded only from ground combat roles, and from submarines and some diving roles.[1] It was decided that the remaining restrictions should be reviewed in about two to three years' time.

To facilitate that review, it was decided that the MOD should carry out a detailed study into the performance and suitability of women in close-combat roles. This work has now been completed and the report entitled *Women in the Armed Forces* made public.

Taking into account the findings of the study, the Secretary of State for Defence announced on 22 May 2002 that the case for lifting the current restrictions on women serving in close-combat roles had not been made. This sets out the background and rationale for that decision.

absolutely essential contribution to the skills, attitudes and effectiveness of our forces.

We are committed to ensuring that more and more women take advantage of the wide range of military careers open to them.

British military doctrine

The Armed Forces are raised, structured and equipped principally for combat. They are to be capable of intervening effectively at short notice in any type of conflict short of general war. They train therefore for high intensity warfare, and adapt for operations at lower levels. It has been the experience of British Armed Forces in recent years that units deployed on operations other than war may also have to engage in direct combat without warning. There is, therefore, an ever-present risk of involvement in high intensity combat.

Current exclusions

The principal areas from which women are excluded today – and which were the concern of this review – are those that are required deliberately to close with and kill the enemy face-to-face, that is, the Royal Marines General Service, Household Cavalry and Royal Armoured Corps, Infantry and the Royal Air Force Regiment. Although there are differences between the forces, all operate in small teams of which the basic component is often the four-person fire team, which may have to face the enemy at close range. This environment poses extraordinary demands on the individuals, and success or failure – and survival – depend upon the cohesion of the team in extreme circumstances for which there are no direct comparators in civilian or even Service life.

Experiences in other countries

In considering whether to change the current position, account was taken of the experience of other countries. In recent history only the former Soviet Union (in World War Two) and Israel (1948 War) have used women in the close combat roles. Both abandoned the practice after the end of the war in question. Currently, some countries permit women to apply to serve in such roles, but have not tested them in combat. Those countries, such as the United Kingdom and the United States, which optimise their forces for high intensity warfare, have generally not opened close-combat roles to women, or have placed restrictions on how they can be deployed.

The key considerations

The *Women in the Armed Forces* study was conducted to get a better understanding of the impact of employing women in the most demanding close-combat roles. It included a survey of the scientific literature available, a review of the physical selection standards for recruits, an opinion survey conducted amongst the Armed Forces and their families, and the results of a field exercise to explore the impact of mixed-gender teams on cohesion and military performance. Careful consideration was given to the available evidence on the impact of including women in front-line units. Existing data and new research on the comparative physical performance of men and women in a military context, the psychological differences which impact on performance in close combat, the dynamics of mixed and single-sex teams and the legal and ethical issues surrounding equality and diversity in the Armed Forces, were amongst the factors considered.

Physiological factors

The physical capacities demanded of personnel serving in close-combat roles are necessarily high. Any reduction in standards would pose unacceptable risks to the operational effectiveness of our forces, and must therefore be avoided. The physical tests taken by potential recruits measure their ability to carry out the tasks that they will be required to perform after appropriate training. The testing standards that are set are justified by the demands of the job.

The *Women in the Armed Forces* report examined the differences in the physical abilities of men and women which are relevant to military performance and observed, unsurprisingly, that they differ significantly. Differences between women and men in their capacity to develop muscle strength and aerobic fitness are such that only approximately 1% of women can equal the performance of the average man. In lifting, carrying and similar tasks performed routinely by the British Army, this means that, on average, women have a lower work capacity than men and, when exposed to the same physical workload as men, have to work 50-80% harder to achieve the same results. This puts them at greater risk of injury. In load marching, another fundamental military task, and in all other simulated combat tasks, women were found to perform worse than men, and the greater the load, the greater the discrepancy. The study concluded that about 0.1% of female applicants and 1% of trained female soldiers would reach the required standards to meet the demands of these roles.

Psychological factors

The report found that few of the psychological differences between men and women could be said to have a significant bearing on their respective suitability for close-combat roles. The capacity for aggression, however, was generally lower for women, who required more provocation and were more likely to fear consequences of aggressive behaviour. There was evidence though that this gap could be closed given sufficient social licence and provocation.

Combat effectiveness

Critical to combat effectiveness is the ability of a unit, formation, ship or weapon system to carry out its assigned mission. Infantry and armoured units operate primarily in small units as fire teams or individual tank crews and the maintenance of cohesion amongst the team members is a vital component in sustaining combat effectiveness. There is some evidence from the literature survey that the inclusion of small numbers of women adds to the difficulty of creating the necessary degree of cohesion. It found that the attitudes of group members, particularly positive and negative attitudes to gender and gender stereotypes, could affect group dynamics and ultimately group effectiveness. The *Women in the Armed Forces* report observed that it might be easier to achieve and maintain cohesion in a single-sex team.

Other evidence however suggests that, under normal conditions (that is the difficult and arduous conditions of operations other than war but not warfighting) and given proper management and training, the presence of women in small units does not affect performance detrimentally. However, the studies reviewed were not based on combat situations and there is no evidence to show whether this remains true under the extreme conditions of high intensity close combat. The reality of warfighting is that the combat team must function effectively over an extended period in conditions that are characterised by extreme danger, confusion, fatigue and noise. There is no way of knowing whether mixed-gender teams can function as well as all-male teams in a close-combat environment. Empirical evidence on this subject cannot be obtained, as there is no way to replicate the conditions of close combat by any means short of risking our forces in battle.

Legal position

The Sex Discrimination Act (1975) allows the Armed Forces to exclude women from those posts where the military judgement is that the employment of women would undermine and degrade combat effectiveness. This policy was upheld by the European Court of Justice in October 1999, which ruled in *Sirdar versus the Army Board and the Secretary of State* that the Equal Treatment Directive did not preclude the exclusion of women from certain posts in the Armed Forces, where such exclusions were necessary and appropriate to ensure operational effectiveness, but there was a duty to assess periodically the activities concerned in order to decide whether, in the light of social developments, the derogation from the general scheme of the Directive may still be maintained.

Reasons for the decision

The Secretary of State is satisfied that as some women will certainly be able to meet the standard required of personnel performing in close-combat roles, the evidence of women's lower physical capacity should not, in itself, be a reason to maintain the restrictions. Nor are the identified psychological differences between men and women, or the gap in the capacity for aggression, compelling evidence that women would perform less well in close combat.

The key issue is the potential impact of gender mixing in the small teams essential to success in the close-combat environment. The small size of the basic unit in ground combat, coupled with the unrelenting mental and physical pressure extending over days or weeks, sets them apart from other military roles. Even small failures in a high-intensity close-combat environment can lead to loss

---

Future developments

The Government is committed to promoting equality of opportunity. The Ministry of Defence and the Armed Forces will continue to work closely with the Equal Opportunities Commission and share with them the results of further work to examine the wider issues raised by this study. Women must have the opportunities to progress to the highest ranks, and if they are to do so ways need to be found to retain more women for longer. Ways in which the unique and demanding conditions of Service life, including the unlimited liability to deploy at short notice, can be better reconciled with the demands of family life will continue to be examined. These conflicting demands affect men also, but most often bear disproportionately on women. The Armed Forces will continue to develop training regimes that will unlock the potential of every individual whilst taking into account the differing physiological capacities of men and women that the report highlights. A better understanding will be sought of the impact of team cohesion in those roles in which men and women work together. Finally, terms of service will be examined that offer greater flexibility of employment, but without jeopardising overall levels of operational effectiveness.

---

of life or the failure of the team to meet its objectives. None of the work that either has been, or could be, done can illuminate the key question of the impact of gender mixing on the combat team in close-combat conditions.

Given the lack of direct evidence, from either field exercises or from the experience of other countries, the Secretary of State concluded that military judgement must form the basis of any decision. The military viewpoint was that under the conditions of a high intensity close-quarter battle, group cohesion becomes of much greater significance to team performance and, in such an environment, the consequences of failure can have far-reaching and grave consequences. To admit women would, therefore, involve a risk with no gains in terms of combat effectiveness to offset it.

The above arguments have been considered in relation to each of the units and roles in question – the Royal Marines General Service, Household Cavalry and Royal Armoured Corps, Infantry and the

---

The key issue is the potential impact of gender mixing in the small teams essential to success in the close-combat environment

---

RAF Regiment – to decide whether or not they apply equally to them all. As all the roles necessitate individuals working together in small teams which have to face and engage the enemy at close range, the Secretary of State for Defence concluded that the case for lifting the current restrictions on women serving in combat roles has not been made for any of the units in question. Taking the risk that the inclusion of women in close combat teams could adversely affect those units in the extraordinary circumstances of high intensity close-combat cannot be justified.

This Document reflects Ministry of Defence Service Personnel Policy as at May 2002. Any enquiries on the Service Personnel Policy contained herein should be addressed to: Directorate of Service Personnel Policy Service Conditions, Ministry of Defence, Room 673, St Giles Court, 1-13 St Giles High Street, London, WC2H 8LD.

Reference

1 Women may not serve on submarines or as mine clearance divers for medical reasons. These restrictions were the subject of a separate review and are not considered further here.

■ The above information is from the Ministry of Defence's web site which can be found at www.mod.uk

Women still barred from frontline military duties

Practical test of female capacity in close combat could not be justified, defence secretary rules as report's findings are disclosed

By Richard Norton-Taylor

Women will continue to be barred from close combat roles in the armed forces because it would be too risky to find out how their presence would affect operations, Geoff Hoon, the defence secretary, said yesterday.

A long-awaited report on women in the forces refers to their lower physical capacity and psychological differences from men, including a 'gap in the capacity for aggression'.

However, these were not conclusive, the report said. The key factor was the potential threat to the combat effectiveness and cohesion of four-member teams required 'to close with and kill the enemy face to face'.

The only way of knowing whether that threat was real or illusory would be to experiment in real combat. Mr Hoon was not prepared to risk lives by exposing mixed-gender teams to combat, a defence official said.

Mr Hoon is known to have had doubts about the implacable opposition among military chiefs to any change in the existing rules but he did not want to pick a fight with them on the issue.

The detailed report – announced through a written parliamentary answer and thus preventing Labour backbenchers from responding – said: 'Given the lack of direct evidence from either field exercises or from the experience of other countries, [Mr Hoon] concluded that military judgement must form the basis of any decision.'

Differences between women and men in their capacity to develop muscle strength and aerobic fitness were such that only about 1% of women could equal the performance of the average man, said the report. When exposed to the same physical workload, women had to work up to 80% harder than men to achieve the same results.

The report also found that 'capacity for aggression . . . was generally lower for women, who required more provocation and were more likely to fear consequences of aggressive behaviour'.

It said there was no way of knowing whether mixed-gender teams of combat troops could cope as well as all-male ones in conditions characterised by extreme danger, confusion, fatigue and noise. But to find out would involve risks which could not be justified.

The decision was criticised by the Equal Opportunities Commission. Jenny Watson, the deputy chairwoman, said the EOC still believed that 'automatically excluding women from armed combat posts is not the right approach and that mixed units would not have a negative impact on operational effectiveness'.

She added: 'Each individual should be judged on the basis of their ability to carry out the job, using relevant tests. It may be that relatively few women would make it through. But that is not a good reason

for denying all women the opportunity to apply.'

Paul Keetch, the Liberal Democrat defence spokesman, said the rigorous standards required for frontline roles should not be compromised. 'But as a matter of principle, no post should be closed to male or female personnel provided they can meet the physical and mental requirements of the task.'

The MoD's report pointed out that the EU's court of justice in 1999 upheld the Ministry of Defence view that the 1975 Sex Discrimination Act and European equal treatment directive could exclude women from close combat roles. However, a new legal challenge is widely expected.

Defence officials insisted yesterday that 'old arguments about chivalry' played no part in the decision and that women had had a 'civilising effect' on the armed forces and had improved discipline on board Royal Navy ships. Sir Michael Boyce, chief of the defence staff, said last year he had 'no problem' with the prospect of women dying on the battlefield but made clear that his main concern was that women infantry, wounded or killed in battle, would affect their male colleagues in a way that would disrupt military operations.

Women are able to serve in 70% of posts in the army, 73% in the navy, and 96% in the RAF, including fast jet pilots. However, they make up only about 8% of the armed forces, and yesterday's report promised more work on how to promote the careers of women in the services.

It said that in recent history only the Soviet Union, in the second world war, and Israel, in its 1948 war, had used women in close combat roles but both had later abandoned the practice.

© *Guardian Newspapers Limited 2002*

Changing relationships between women and men

Towards a new contract between the sexes

The facts

The double lives of women

Thanks to the fight for women's rights, to their increasing participation in the job market, to women's right to vote, to the generalised use of contraception (which allows women to chose whether and when to have children), women have emerged from the strictly private, family sphere to which they were formerly restricted. Women have broken the implicit social contract that for hundreds of years confined them to the home, to child rearing, to household tasks and to field work, while men worked outside the home.

But while women have won the right to be citizens and workers, the traditional division of tasks in the workplace and the home still applies, even within young couples.

Women cannot afford to be content with these achievements. They have careers, jobs, professional responsibilities, but continue to be in large part responsible for their children, household chores and care of dependants (whose needs are increasing as the population ages). Many women therefore, have to combine a full-time job with a full-time family life.

In addition to the technical problems involved in carrying this

---

Women perform 80% of household tasks and they spend nearly twice as much time as men in child care

---

'double burden', such as the shortage of affordable child care and the need in many cases to work part-time, young women often express a real fear of not being up to either job. Whether they fear 'sacrificing' their children to their careers or fear having to give up their careers to be 'good mothers', women face heavy responsibilities and pressures that their partners do not.

A few statistics

- In nine out of ten single-parent families, the parent is a woman;[1]
- Men who take parental leave are the exception: 7 men per 100 women in Denmark in 1995, 1 man per 100 women in France in 1992, and 2 women per 100 men in Germany in 1995;[2]
- Women perform 80% of household tasks (except in Nordic countries), they spend nearly twice as much time as men in child care (41 hours/week compared with 21)[3]
- The employment rate of women with at least 1 child is 53% and of women without children is 68%.[4]

The new family

One of the keys to the problem is the perception of the family. Family policy and legislation is often ill adapted to new types of families, including single-parent families, separated families, and single-sex couples raising children. Young women identify the need to redefine the family and the couple, with a more flexible and more tolerant approach. Young women also reflected on the need to involve young men in the definition of the future of equality. The debate will not be possible without them. They recognised that men are also subject to social pressure that limits their participation in this type of debate.

The law

European legislation offers a number of solutions to help reconcile family and working life:

Child care

A recommendation by the Council of Ministers, the body representing the governments of the EU Member States, addresses the issue of child

---

care and supports initiatives that help women as well as men combine professional activity and child care.

Parental leave
A directive provides for a minimum of three months of parental leave for men as well as women upon the birth or adoption of a child.

Pregnant women
A 1992 directive sets out a series of minimum requirements for improvements to safety and health in the workplace for pregnant women, those who have just given birth or are breastfeeding and provides for paid maternity leave as well as protection against being made redundant.

Young women's ideas
Young women's priority is to establish a new contract between women and men to allow everyone to participate

---

Young women also reflected on the need to involve young men in the definition of the future of equality. The debate will not be possible without them

---

fully and completely, on an equal footing, in all areas. This will require:
- A new definition of the role of women and men in society.
- Encouragement for part-time work (by choice), paid parental leave shared between mother and father, the provision by the Member States of affordable, high-quality child care for children and assistance for dependent persons, and the reduction of

working time to facilitate combining work and family.
- Assessment of the economic value of women's work in the home to make this 'invisible' work visible.

References

1 *Single-parent families in the European Community*, European Commission, 1992.
2 *Annual Report on Equal Opportunities for Women and Men in the EU 1995*, European Commission.
3 *The social situation in the EU*, Eurostat, 2000.
4 Eurostat 1998, *Labour Force Survey*.

■ The above information is an extract from *Young Women's Guide to Equality between Women and Men in Europe*, a publication by the European Women's Lobby. See page 41 for their address details or visit their web site: www.womenlobby.org

Working fathers

Dads do a third of childcare but don't get flexibility at work

British dads do approximately a third of all childcare but don't get the flexibility they need at work to help them do more. Our working culture, where long hours are the norm for many, prevents dads from being more involved with their children's lives, even though they want to be, according to a new report published today by the Equal Opportunities Commission (EOC).

Working Fathers: Earning and Caring, carried out by Margaret O'Brien and Ian Shemilt of the University of East Anglia, found high support for work-life balance among fathers as well as mothers. However, fathers have lower expectations of family-friendly working practices being available to them personally and are less likely to take advantage of those that are in place.

Nearly two-fifths of fathers usually work more than 48 hours a week and around one in eight usually work 60 hours or more. Satisfaction with work-life balance is much lower for these fathers than for those working more reasonable hours. The

Women. Men. Different. Equal.
Equal Opportunities Commission

time fathers spend with their children accounts for approximately one-third of the total parental childcare time, but the long-hours culture prevents a more equal sharing of caring.

Julie Mellor, Chair of the EOC, said: 'Many dads are spending far more time with their family than

---

Dads are already doing around a third of all childcare and the vast majority of all parents believe everyone should be able to balance their work and home lives in the way that they want

---

their own fathers did, but it is difficult for them to do more while they work such long hours. The knock-on effect is that women often have little choice about how they balance work and family.

'However, dads are already doing around a third of all childcare and the vast majority of all parents believe everyone should be able to balance their work and home lives in the way that they want. The new right for parents of young children to ask to change their working hours seems certain to be welcomed by many men as well as women.'

The report draws attention to the higher involvement of fathers whose partners work full-time, or whose partners have a high income, which suggests that cash v. care negotiation happens in many families.

Evidence from other recent EOC research reinforces this, showing that because women earn less, couples often decide it makes economic sense for the woman to give up work or cut her hours so she

Satisfaction with work-life balance dropped to 60% for men working more than 48 hours a week and to 50% for those working more than 60 hours a week

can care for the children; and so women continue to earn less and the caring role is still seen primarily as a female one.

Julie Mellor added: 'Employers can help break this cycle by making sure they promote their family-friendly working practices to all their employees, as well as reviewing their pay systems to ensure they are paying women fairly. This is in employers' interests and the interests of the economy as a whole, as it can boost morale and productivity.'

This research also cites the experience of the Nordic countries where governments have found that fathers are more likely to take parental leave under four key conditions: where it includes a quota designated for fathers, where there is high wage compensation, where there is flexibility in the way leave can be used by couples and where male provision is publicised through government awareness campaigns.

Other findings

In the mid 1970s fathers of children under 5 devoted less than a quarter of an hour per day to child-related activities, compared to two hours a day by the late 1990s.

80% of fathers and 85% of mothers, compared to 62% of employers, agreed everyone should be able to balance their work and home lives in the way they want. However, fathers' expectations about whether they would have access to specific work-life balance practices were lower than mothers'.

Fathers did have higher expectations about being able to take paternity leave or have time off if a child was sick – expectations not matched by the actual availability of leave.

Fathers' use of flexible working is lower than mothers' in every category except shift work and working from home.

Eight out of ten employers felt work-life balance practices fostered good employment relations and two-thirds agreed that they improved staff motivation, commitment, retention and turnover.

Yet more than half of employers did not offer any form of flexible working.

Less than 10% of fathers had access to a crèche, subsidised nursery place or financial help with childcare. More than half had access to workplace counselling or stress management advice.

- 61% of fathers with a child under the age of one had taken paternity leave in the last year. Fathers in non-manual occupations were more likely to take paternity leave.
- Satisfaction with work-life balance dropped to 60% for men working more than 48 hours a week and to 50% for those working more than 60 hours a week.

Notes

1. *Working Fathers: Earning and Caring*, provides a review of recent literature on working fathers and a secondary analysis of two DfEE Work-Life Balance Surveys carried out in 2000. The Employee Survey was a nationally representative sample of 7,500 employed persons in employment in workplaces with five or more staff and the Employers Survey was a nationally representa-tive sample of 2,500 workplaces with five or more staff. Interviews were conducted by telephone between April and June 2000.

2. The EOC also recently published *Dads on Dads*, which found that although dads play a range of roles in the family most still regard themselves primarily as bread-winners. It found that women's lower average pay is a key factor in maintaining traditional gender roles in many families. Other factors that affect dads' involve-ment in the family include a lack of confidence in their own caring skills and a working culture of long and inflexible hours.

3. From 6 April 2003 employers will have a legal duty to consider requests for flexible working from employees who are parents of young children. To be eligible to make a request, employees must have parental responsibility for a child aged under six or for a disabled child aged under 18.

4. Fathers will have the right to two weeks paid paternity leave within 8 weeks' of the child's birth, paid at the same rate as standard maternity pay. Paid maternity leave will be extended to 26 weeks, and unpaid maternity leave will also be extended to 26 weeks. The standard rate of maternity pay will increase to £100 per week (or 90% of weekly earnings if this is less).

- The above information is from the Equal Opportunities Commission's web site which can be found at www.eoc.org.uk

© 2003 Equal Opportunities Commission

Home truths

Introduction

This briefing outlines the initial findings from a Fawcett and British Banker's Association research project, which looks at financial decision making within households. The data comes from various editions[1] of the British Household Panel Survey (BHPS) and has been analysed by the Institute for Social and Economic Research, University of Essex, Colchester.

Key findings

Women's income
- Half of women surveyed have an income of under £800 a month compared to 20% of men.

Financial decision making
- Most couples share financial decision making. However, a fifth of women say their husband/partner has the final say.
- Access to decision making is associated with personal income, women with higher personal incomes are more likely than those with low incomes to say they make their decisions jointly.
- 24% of women with personal incomes of less than £400 a month said their husband/partner made big financial decisions compared with 12% of women with an income between £1200 and £1600.

Systems of finance management
- Joint financial management systems were reported where women had a higher personal income.
- Female management of day-to-day finances were associated with lower income households.

Responsibility for household bills
- Paying household bills is seen as primarily a female task. 42% of men and 47% of women said that the woman was responsible for paying the bills.
- Responsibility for household bills is more likely to be reported as the man's task where he personally or the household as a whole has a higher income.

24% of women with personal incomes of less than £400 a month said their husband/partner made big financial decisions

---

Joint bank accounts
- Likelihood of having a joint bank account is associated with individual and household income.
- Men with low personal income were less likely than men with a high personal income to have a joint account with their partner.

Wealth and savings
- Women in higher income households are more likely to have independent access to savings than women in low income households.
- Older men are more likely than younger men to have savings in joint names.
- Women were less likely to save overall, but more likely than men within the same personal income range to have savings.

Reference
1 Data comes from BHPS carried out between 1991-1999. In all cases the most recent figures have been used

- The above information is an extract from *Home Truths*, a report produced by the Fawcett Society, see page 41 for their address details.
  © *Fawcett Society*

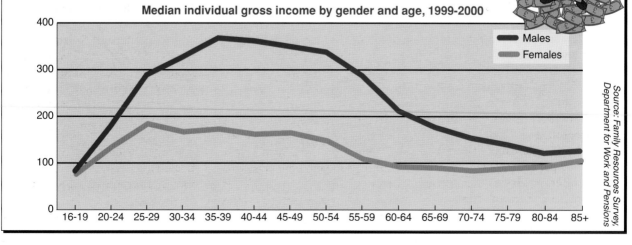

Gross income

Men's incomes outstripped those of women in all age groups in 1999-2000: the median gross income of women was 49 per cent of that of men. However, the gap varied according to age. In the youngest age group, incomes were very close (£83 per week for 16- to 19-year-old males, £76 per week for females). For women aged between 35 and 64, incomes were less than half those of men of the same age.

Median individual gross income by gender and age, 1999-2000

— Males
— Females

Source: Family Resources Survey, Department for Work and Pensions

Breaking free from sex stereotyping

Stereotypes pigeonhole boys and girls, men and women into fixed roles and behaviours that deny individual aspirations. Although women now make up half the British workforce, the old assumption that men should be earning a living while women are at home looking after the house and family continues to restrict opportunities for both sexes.

Examples

- Children express fixed views about men's and women's roles at a very early age. In a survey of primary school age children, 95 per cent of boys thought that car repairs should only be done by men, and 85 per cent of girls thought that washing and mending clothes should only be done by women.
- 90 per cent of students who took Foundation General National Vocational Qualification (GNVQ) in health and social care in 2001 were female, 81 per cent of those taking IT were male. Young people are choosing subjects according to traditional stereotypes which will limit their options for the future.
- The divide continues at A'level: 74 per cent of students who took English in 2001 were female, 72 per cent of those taking computing were male.

Segregation in the workplace

- engineering apprenticeships: 96 per cent men
- health and social care apprenticeships: 89 per cent women
- computer analysts and programmers: 79 per cent men
- primary and nursery teachers: 86 per cent women

Women. Men. Different. Equal.
Equal Opportunities Commission

The cost

Discrimination
Individual men and women who go against the grain face restricted job opportunities, isolation and harassment.

Wasted talent
Young people cannot fulfil their potential unless all subjects are realistic options to them. Stereotypes limit the individual ambitions of both girls and boys.

Skills gaps
Some industries with skills shortages are recruiting from a restricted pool. There is a skills shortage in the computer industry yet the number of women entering this industry is falling.

Unequal pay
Women in Britain working full-time earn on average 19% less than men. One of the reasons for this pay gap is the concentration of women in certain types of jobs, which attract less money than jobs traditionally done by men

Disaffection
Masculine stereotypes which glamorise 'laddish' behaviour have a negative effect on boys' performance at school.

EOC campaign

- To raise awareness of the extent of stereotyping through research
- Demonstrate the damage it causes through targeted publicity campaigns
- Lobby government to address gender stereotypes in education and training
- Work with employers to address fixed ideas about men's and women's jobs
- Promote good practice.

What others can do

Schools
Set targets for boys and girls in different subjects, promote positive role models of men and women doing non-stereotypical jobs, introduce discussion of gender roles into Personal, Health and Social Education.

Careers advisers
Give comprehensive advice about different options. Encourage diverse work placements. Involve employers as mentors and role models.

Parents
Encourage children to learn wide variety of subjects, regardless of their sex.

Government
Promote positive action by starting a Challenge Fund for schools who want to promote diversity. Introduce gender awareness into the curriculum for Citizenship Education, and for teacher training.

Employers
Promote their sector to people of both sexes. Introduce mentoring schemes to support individuals in a minority, and training for managers to root out discrimination.

Find out more

The EOC's *What's Stopping You?* Campaign pack includes more information and resources to tackle sex stereotypes in education and training.

- The above information is from the Equal Opportunities Commission's web site which can be found at www.eoc.org.uk

© 2003 *Equal Opportunities Commission*

European legislation on equality between women and men

Europe as a role model for equality

The facts

Europe broadens the concept of equality

The European Union is not merely a common market; its development is synonymous with a more 'social' Union. Since the creation of the European Communities in 1957, legislation on equality between women and men has made extensive progress, which started out to guarantee equal pay between women and men and now extends to cover all forms of sexual discrimination in the workplace.

Impact on daily life

The scope of the Union's activities in all its areas of competence is so broad that they directly influence women's daily lives. Moreover, in the areas where Member States have given the EU the power to act, European laws take precedence over national legislation, and a national law that contravenes European law has to be changed. In other terms, if progress is made at European level, it must be incorporated at national level. As European legislation sometimes goes a step further than national legislation in equality of opportunity between women and men, it is essential for young women to be informed of the possibilities the European Union has to offer and to participate in programmes introduced by the Union.

The law

The treaties

Equal pay in the Treaty of Rome (1957)

The first important piece of legislation relating to equality in the first Community legal texts was contained in Article 119 of the Treaty of Rome, which introduced the principle of equal pay for women and men for equal work. This principle was used extensively by the European Court of Justice to ensure equal opportunities between women and men in the labour market in general.

Discrimination based on sex in the Treaty of Amsterdam

In 1997, the principle of equality between women and men, extending beyond the issue of pay, was introduced for the first time into the European Treaties as one of the basic objectives of the Community (Articles 2 and 3 of the Treaty of Amsterdam). Article 13 of the same Treaty, which is an article on discrimination, in general, also makes reference to discrimination on grounds of sex. This is one of the European Women's Lobby's great victories: the progress achieved in this instance was partly due to the lobbying efforts of many women across Europe.

Reference to equal pay in the Treaty of Amsterdam

Article 141 of the Treaty of Amsterdam contains a reference to equal pay for women and men for equal work or work of equal value and also introduces positive action measures.

Directives

Directives are 'laws' adopted at European level, which must be transposed into national legislation in all of the Member States (a national law that contravenes a Directive must be changed).

The main Directives on gender equality are:

- Equal pay (1975)

Young women have specific ideas for making full use of and developing European legislation on equality

- Equal treatment relating to employment, vocational training, promotion and general working conditions (1976)
- Social security systems (1978 and 1986)
- Equal treatment for self-employed workers and their spouses (1986)
- Pregnancy and motherhood (1992)
- Parental leave (1996)
- Burden of proof in cases of sex discrimination (1998).

The European Charter of Fundamental Rights

The European Charter of Fundamental Rights was proclaimed in December 2000, but its legal status is still uncertain. While reference is made to discrimination against women, overall its reference to a prohibition of discrimination against women is insufficient.

International law

The Member States of the European Union are also bound to commitments of international law passed by other institutions. These take precedence over national law, as well, such as:

(The right to) the enjoyment of fundamental rights without discrimination (including sex discrimination) in the European Convention of Human Rights of 1953.

(The right to) equal access for women and men and equal opportunity in politics and public life, education and employment in the UN Convention on the Elimination of all forms of Discrimination Against Women (CEDAW) of 1981.

UN conferences on women like the Beijing Conference of 1995 also help to promote sexual equality around the world.

Young women's ideas

Young women have specific ideas for making full use of and developing European legislation on equality by:

- Taking advantage of the legislative opportunities provided in the Treaty of Amsterdam.
- Initiating campaigns to increase public awareness of equality between women and men.
- Creating youth councils composed of equal numbers of girls and boys to advise governments at local, national and European level.
- Informing young women about existing legislation and other awareness raising activities.

■ The above information is an extract from *Young Women's Guide to Equality between Women and Men in Europe*, by the European Women's Lobby. For more details visit their web site: www.womenlobby.org
© *European Women's Lobby*

Key indicators of women's position in Britain

By Sally Dench, Jane Aston, Ceri Evans, Nigel Meager, Matthew Williams and Rebecca Willison (Institute for Employment Studies)

Key findings

- In 2001, there were around 30.4 million women in the UK and 29.6 million men: women account for 51% of the population.
- Women have a longer life expectancy than men. Life expectancy for both sexes has been increasing, although the difference between them has narrowed slightly in recent years.
- Women's economic activity has been increasing over the last ten years, whereas men's has been decreasing over the same period. The gender gap in employment rates has also narrowed.
- However, there are still far fewer women than men in managerial occupations: only 8% of all women in employment are managers, compared with 18% of men.
- Women are more and more likely to return to work after childbirth: the proportion doing so has increased from 45% in 1988 to 67% in 1996. The proportion returning to work full-time has also gone up.
- Availability of childcare places has been increasing since the second half of the 1990s. This helps women (and men) to balance work and family commitments.
- The gender gap in hourly earnings has narrowed from women earning just 63% of men's hourly earnings in 1970 to 82% in 2000.
- But women are slightly more likely than men to live in low-income households: they make up 55% of all people living in such households.
- Women are more worried about crime than men are, but overall levels of concern have fallen during the late 1990s. They are less likely to be a victim of a violent crime, but are far more likely to experience domestic violence than men are.

Aims of the research

The aim of this project was therefore to identify a set of key indicators for mapping women's position relative to that of men across a wide range of areas, and to draw together reliable and robust statistics from different sources to provide a comprehensive baseline for monitoring progress. It also outlines recent trends in these indicators, so future changes can be put into context.

■ The above information is the summary of a research project by the Women & Equality Unit.
© *Crown copyright*

■ The standards of achievement for all pupils has been rising since the 1980s but because of the differential rates of improvements, girls are still performing better than boys. (p. 5)

■ Boys' underachievement is an international problem. We know for example that in the USA, Australia, Scotland and Holland girls appear to get off to a better start in reading and writing and sustain the advantage in later schooling. (p. 5)

■ Results posted in schools in August 2002 showed girls out-performed their male classmates in almost every subject. (p. 6)

■ They even triumphed in the traditionally male subject of Information Technology, with 64.4 per cent achieving grades A* to C against 55.7 per cent of boys. (p. 6)

■ Girls now gain more A* grades in every subject, apart from maths and physics. (p. 6)

■ The majority of Science subjects are dominated by boys, the majority of Arts subjects by girls, whereas the Social Sciences are more mixed. (p. 7)

■ All Sciences except for Biological Science are dominated by men, whereas all the Arts are dominated by women. As with GCSE, Social Sciences show a mixed gender distribution. (p. 8)

■ From constituting one-third of undergraduates in 1975, women now make up slightly more than one-half. (p. 8)

■ Gender stereotyping is as prevalent at degree level as in other qualification levels. Men are over-represented in Engineering and Technology whereas women are over-represented in Education and the Humanities. (p. 8)

■ The gap separating men and women on the job market remains wide in all countries of the European Union: women have a lower employment rate, are unemployed longer, are paid less and have less secure jobs. (p. 10)

■ Although young women are increasingly choosing typically 'male' professions, they remain over-represented in traditionally 'female' jobs, as secretaries and nurses. (p. 10)

■ In the EU as a whole, women doing the same work as a man are paid only 76% of the gross hourly wage men earn. (p. 10)

■ 83% of part-time workers in the EU are women. (p. 10)

■ When it comes to management, 30% of managers are women yet they earn considerably less than their male counterparts – 24% less per hour. (p. 11)

■ Women are less likely than men to be self-employed – 6.5% of women compared to 15% of men. (p. 13)

■ Women make up just 24% of managers and just under 10% of directors in companies. (p. 13)

■ Of the top 100 companies listed on the stock exchange (FTSE 100), only one has a woman heading it. (p. 13)

■ 90% of the students who took a health and social care vocational qualification in 2001 were female; 81% of those taking IT were male. (p. 13)

■ The number of female managers as a percentage of the total workforce, as measured by the sample, has risen to 30 per cent – more than double the figure recorded six years ago. (p. 15)

■ In 2000/2001 there were 1,210,000 female managers/senior officials in the UK compared with 2,726,000 men. (p. 16)

■ 30 per cent of all women work part-time. (p. 16)

■ The number of women executive directors among Britain's top firms has risen by 50 per cent in the last year. But even with this increase women still made up just 3 per cent of executive directors in the FTSE top 100 firms. (p. 16)

■ Women working full time earn 80% of the hourly rate of a man working full time. (p. 18)

■ Women working part time earn on average 58% of the hourly rate of a man working full time. (p. 18)

■ Women make up 54.4% of classroom teachers in secondary schools but only 27% of secondary head teachers are women. (p. 19)

■ Over the course of their working lives, women lose out to the tune of £250,000 just because they are women. If they have children, they stand to lose another £140,000. (p 28)

You might like to contact the following organisations for further information. Due to the increasing cost of postage, many organisations cannot respond to enquiries unless they receive a stamped, addressed envelope.

Chartered Management Institute
3rd Floor, 2 Savoy Court
Strand, London, WC2R 0EZ
Tel: 020 7497 0580
Fax: 020 7497 0463
E-mail:
publications@managers.org.uk
Web site: www.managers.org.uk
As the champion of management, the Chartered Management Institute shapes and supports the managers of tomorrow. By sharing insights and setting standards in management development, we help to deliver results in a dynamic world.

Equal Opportunities Commission (EOC)
Arndale House, Arndale Centre
Manchester, M4 3EQ
Tel: 0161 833 9244
Fax: 0161 835 1657
E-mail: info@eoc.org.uk
Web site: www.eoc.org.uk
The Equal Opportunities Commission is the leading agency working to eliminate sex discrimination in 21st-century Britain. They campaign to:
- Close the pay gap between women and men
- Make it easier for parents to balance work with family responsibilities
- Increase the number of women in public life
- Break free of male and female stereotypes
- End sexual harassment at work
- Make public services relevant to the differing needs of men and women
- Secure comprehensive equality legislation in Europe, England, Scotland and Wales.

European Women's Lobby (EWL)
18 Rue Hydraulique
B-1210 Brussels
Belgium
Tel: + 32 2 217 90 20
Fax: + 32 2 219 84 51
E-mail: ewl@womenlobby.org
Web site: www.womenlobby.org
The largest co-ordinating body of national and European non-governmental women's organisations in the European Union, with over 2,700 member associations in the 15 Member States.

Fawcett Society
1-3 Berry Street
London, EC1V 0AA
Tel: 020 7253 2598
Fax: 020 7253 2599
E-mail: info@fawcettsociety.org.uk
Web site: www.fawcettsociety.org.uk
Fawcett wants to see women and men equal partners at home, at work and in public life.
They demand a fair deal for women. They believe every woman should have financial security, work-life balance, educational choice, representation, autonomy and equal treatment.

Save the Children
17 Grove Lane
Camberwell
London, SE5 8RD
Tel: 020 7703 5400
Fax: 020 7703 2278
E-mail: enquiries@scfuk.org.uk
Web sites:
www.savethechildren.org.uk,
 www.savethechildren.org.uk/rightonline,
www.savethechildren.org.uk/education, www.beatpoverty.org
Save the Children is the leading UK charity working to create a better world for children. They work in 70 countries helping children in the world's most impoverished communities. Ask for their catalogue.

UNISON
1 Mabledon Place
London, WC1H 9AJ
Tel: 0845 355 0845
Web site: www.unison.org.uk
UNISON is Britain's biggest trade union with over 1.3 million members. Our members are people working in the public services, for private contractors providing public services and the essential utilities. They include frontline staff and managers working full or part time in local authorities, the NHS, the police service, colleges and schools, the electricity, gas and water industries, transport and the voluntary sector. Last year UNISON recruited 148,755 new members – 407 per day.

The Work Foundation
Customer Centre
Quadrant Court
49 Calthorpe Road
Edgbaston, Birmingham, B15 1TH
Tel: 0870 165 6700
Fax: 0870 165 6701
E-mail:
customercentre@theworkfoundation.com
Web site:
www.theworkfoundation.com
An independent, not-for-profit thinktank and consultancy. Through research, campaigning and practical interventions, they aim to improve the productivity and the quality of working life in the UK.
They want to make our workplaces more effective, more successful and more fulfilling. They do this through research and analysis about the changing world of work; consultancy and practical interventions in UK organisations; and by influencing the public conversation about work and working life.

INDEX

Issues   *www.independence.co.uk*

42

ACKNOWLEDGEMENTS

The publisher is grateful for permission to reproduce the following material.

While every care has been taken to trace and acknowledge copyright, the publisher tenders its apology for any accidental infringement or where copyright has proved untraceable. The publisher would be pleased to come to a suitable arrangement in any such case with the rightful owner.

Chapter One: Gender and Education

Gender, © Save the Children, *Young women and education*, © European Women's Lobby, *The lads in a league of their own*, © Telegraph Group Limited, London 2003, *Understanding G & A*, © Crown copyright is reproduced with the permission of Her Majesty's Stationery Office, *The boys are left standing as GCSE gender gap grows*, © The Daily Mail, August 2002, *Gender and education*, © Equal Opportunities Commission (EOC), *Examination results*, © Crown copyright is reproduced with the permission of Her Majesty's Stationery Office.

Chapter Two: Gender and Work

Young women and work, © European Women's Lobby, *Where have all the women gone?*, © Guardian Newspapers Limited 2002, *Give us a job!*, © Crown copyright is reproduced with the permission of Her Majesty's Stationery Office, *Women directors come out on top*, © Chartered Management Institute, *Female managers*, © Chartered Management Institute, *Qualifications*, © Chartered Management Institute, *Women march slowly to the top*, © The Daily Mail, November 2002, *The fight for equal pay*, © The Daily Mail, December 2002, *Equal pay*, © Fawcett Society, *Understanding the gender pay gap*, © Crown copyright is reproduced with the permission of Her Majesty's Stationery Office, *Gender segregation by industrial sector*, © Third European Working Conditions Survey 2000, European Foundation for the Improvement of Living and Working Conditions, *Rising trend in inequality*, © Incomes Data Services (IDS), *Inequality*, © NES/IDS, *Women struggle to join £100k club*, © Guardian Newspapers Limited 2002, *Thin on top!*, © The Work Foundation, *Winning equal pay*, © UNISON, *Mind the gap!*, © Crown copyright is reproduced with the permission of Her Majesty's Stationery Office, *Women in the armed forces*, © Crown Copyright 2002/MOD. Reproduced with the permission of the Controller of Her Majesty's Stationery Office, *Women still barred from frontline military duties*, © Guardian Newspapers Limited 2002.

Chapter Three: Gender Roles

Changing relationships between women and men, © European Women's Lobby, *Working fathers*, © Equal Opportunities Commission (EOC), *Home truths*, © Fawcett Society, *Gross income*, © Family Resources Survey, Department for Work and Pensions/ Crown copyright is reproduced with the permission of Her Majesty's Stationery Office, *Breaking free from sex stereotyping*, © Equal Opportunities Commission (EOC), *European legislation on equality between women and men*, © European Women's Lobby, *Key indicators of women's position in Britain*, © Crown copyright is reproduced with the permission of Her Majesty's Stationery Office.

Photographs and illustrations:

Pages 1, 6, 18, 26, 30, 33, 35, 38: Simon Kneebone; pages 2, 10: Bev Aisbett; pages 4, 14, 28: Pumpkin House.

Craig Donnellan
Cambridge
May, 2003